RAVINA
The Witch?

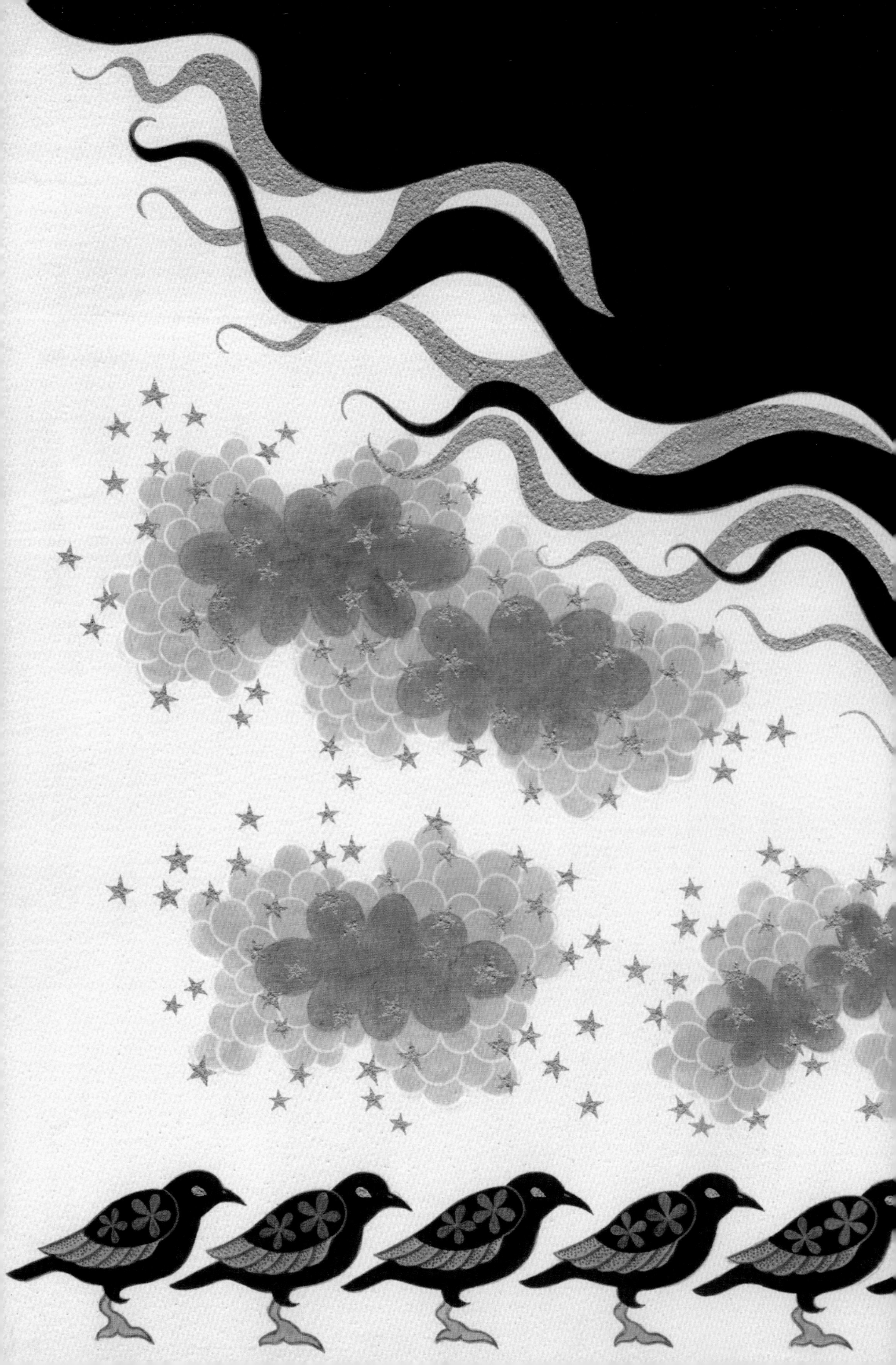

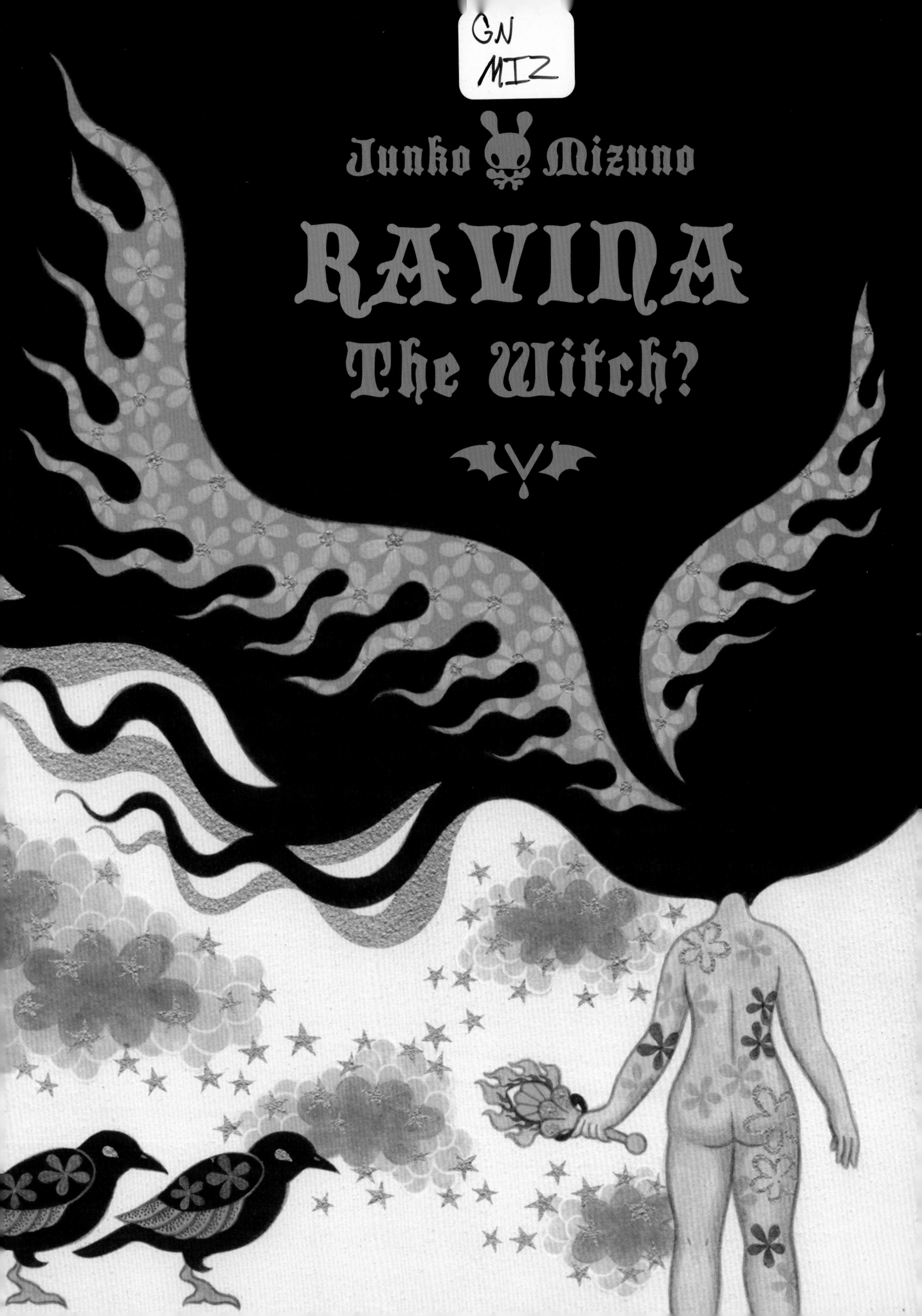
Junko Mizuno
RAVINA
The Witch?

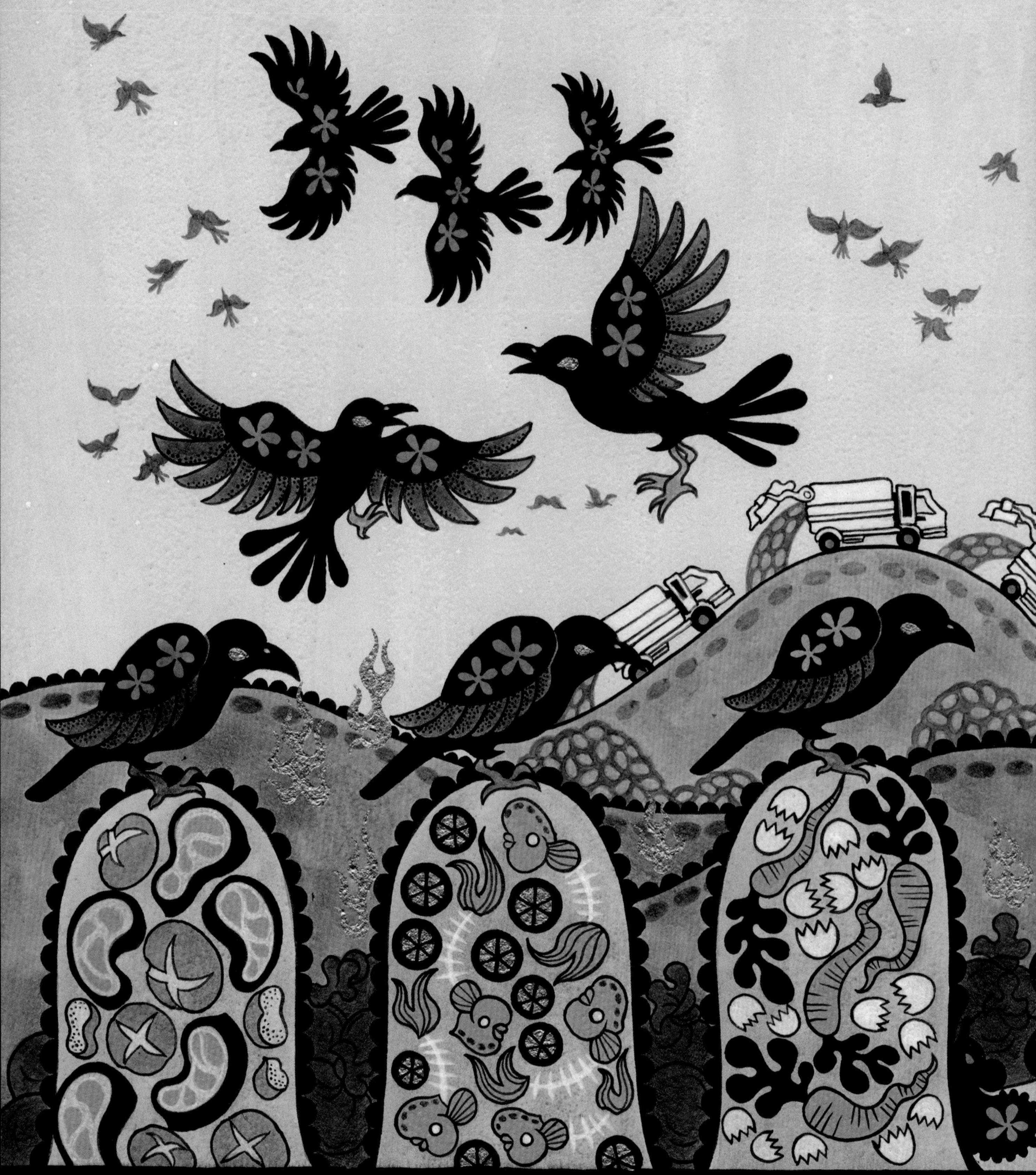

Somewhere, on the coastline of a tiny country in Europe, there was an enormous garbage dump. It kept growing and growing thanks to the many garbage trucks that visited it every day. In this dump, there lived a thousand crows and one human girl.

Her name was Ravina.

Ravina was not sure how she came to live in the dump. It seemed as though she had always been there, raised by the crows. You might think that living in a garbage dump would be miserable, but it's really not so bad at all.

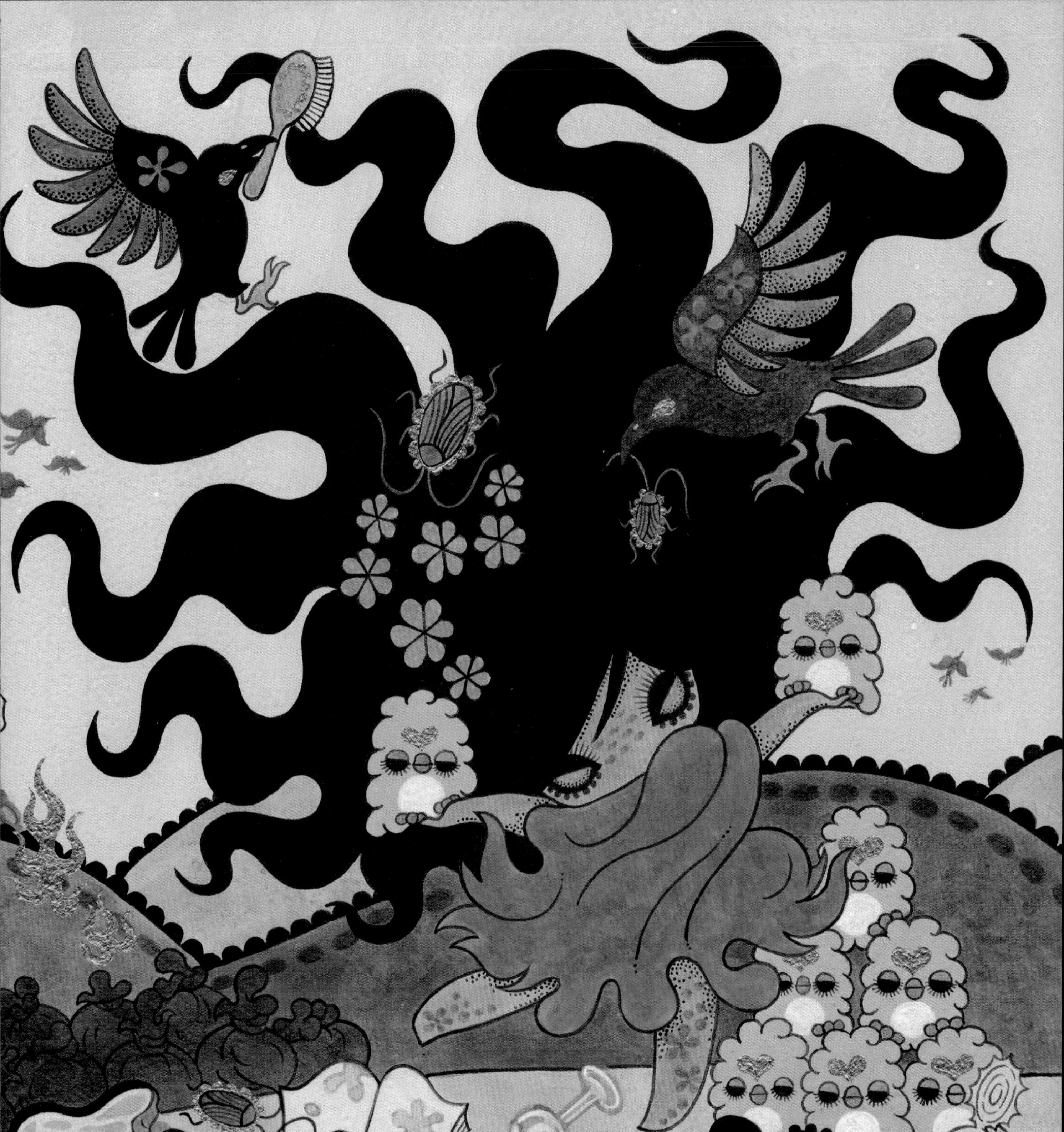

Ravina always had enough to eat. There was lots of food like bread, vegetables, meat, and even a few delicacies no one would expect to find in such a place.

In the dump, Ravina could also find things like picture books, dolls and even the latest toys that had lost their popularity. Ravina didn't care about the smell at all, for it was the only smell she had ever known. She enjoyed her life in the garbage dump and she knew of no other humans... only her family of kindly crows.

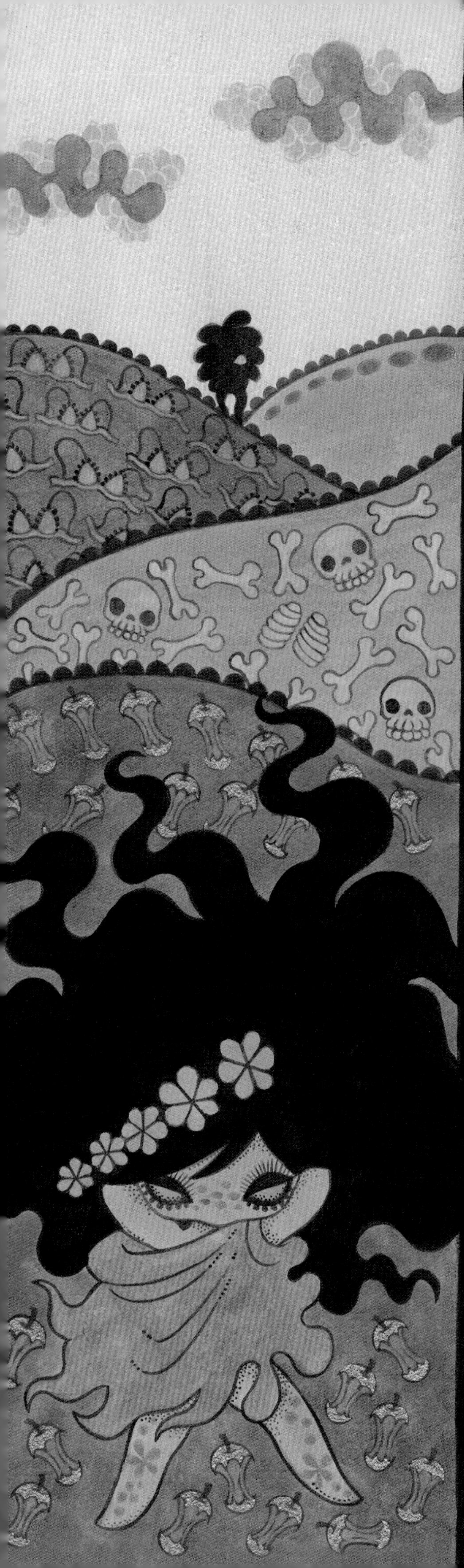

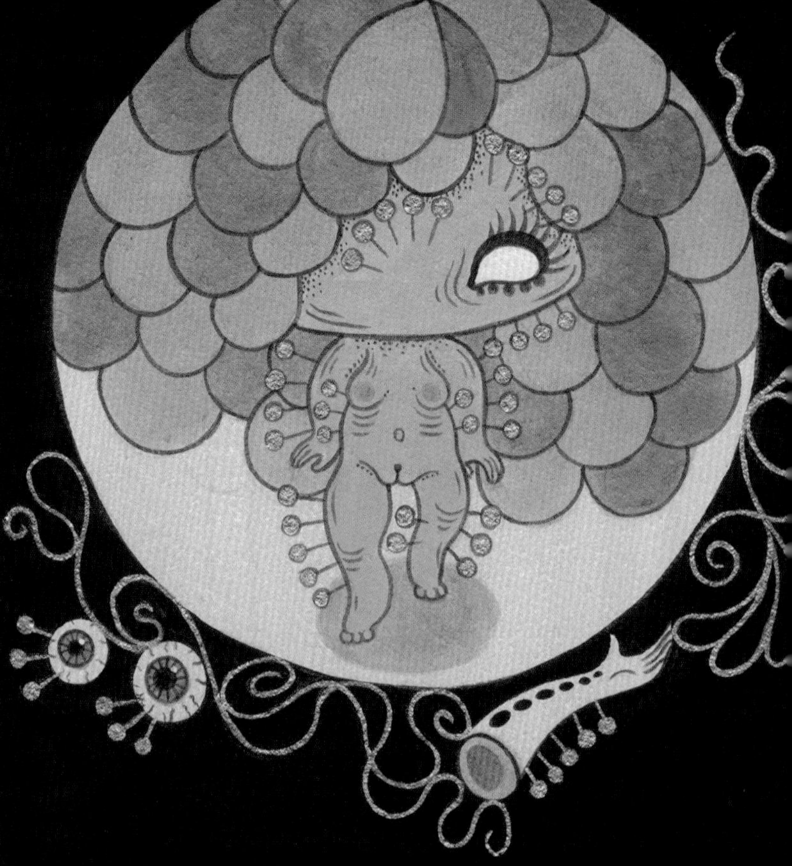

One day, as Ravina stretched out and bathed in the sun, she saw a strange creature walking her way. As the figure came closer, Ravina discovered it was an old woman. She was stumbling along with needles sticking out all over her body.

Ravina was quite surprised. This was the first time she had ever seen another human! But the old woman was in pain, and Ravina took pity on her. She carefully removed all of the needles from her tired old body and helped her to drink some water.

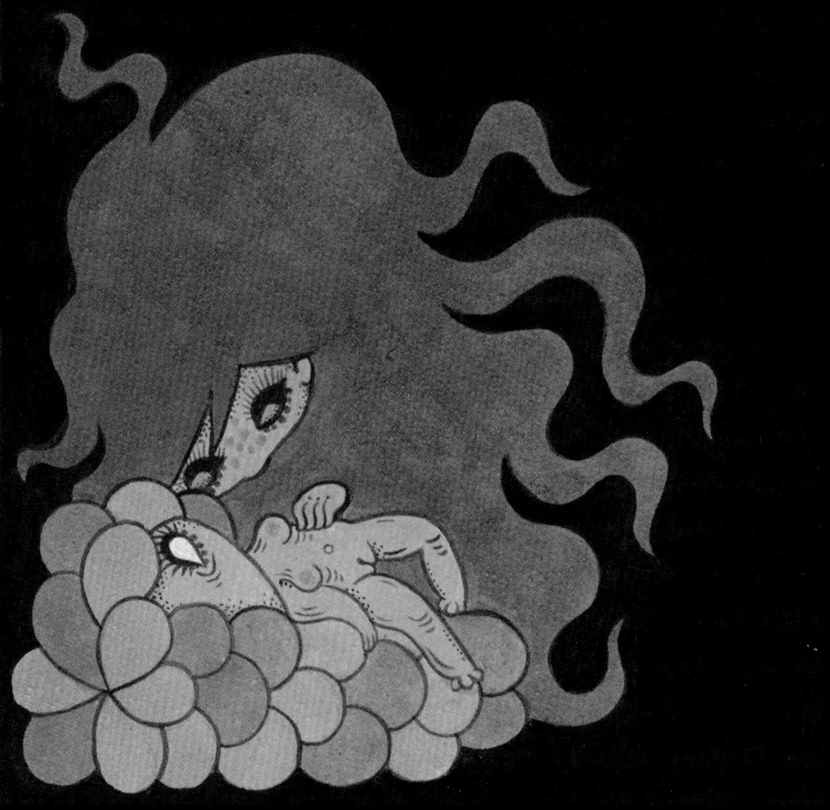

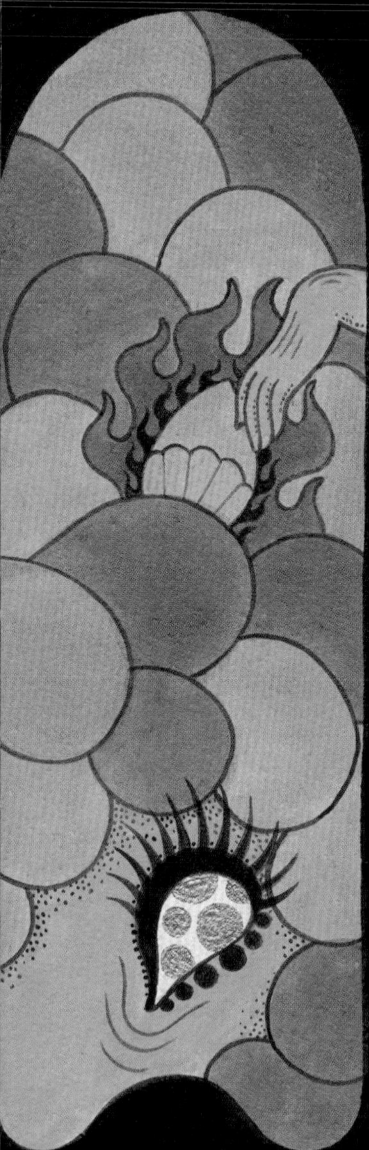

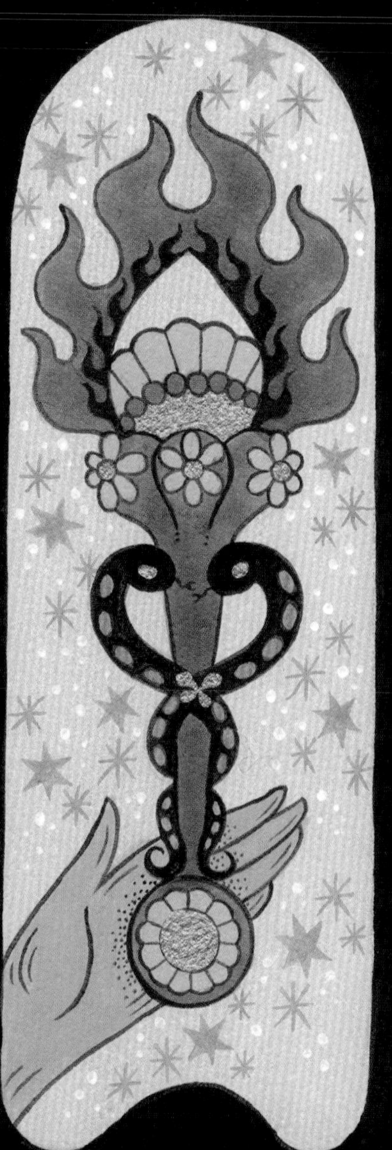

The old woman thanked Ravina for her kindness. In a feeble voice, she explained that she had been accused of being a witch. Because of this, she had been captured and tortured. But eventually, she somehow managed to escape.

The old woman reached into her hair and pulled out a beautiful wand. She handed it to Ravina and said, “They were right. I am a witch. This is my magic wand. I no longer have the power to use it, so I give it to you. To cast a spell, you must always recite these magic words...”

The magic words were spoken... but unfortunately, Ravina couldn’t understand what the old woman was saying at all. She only knew the language of the crows! When the old woman finished the spell, she closed her eyes and died.

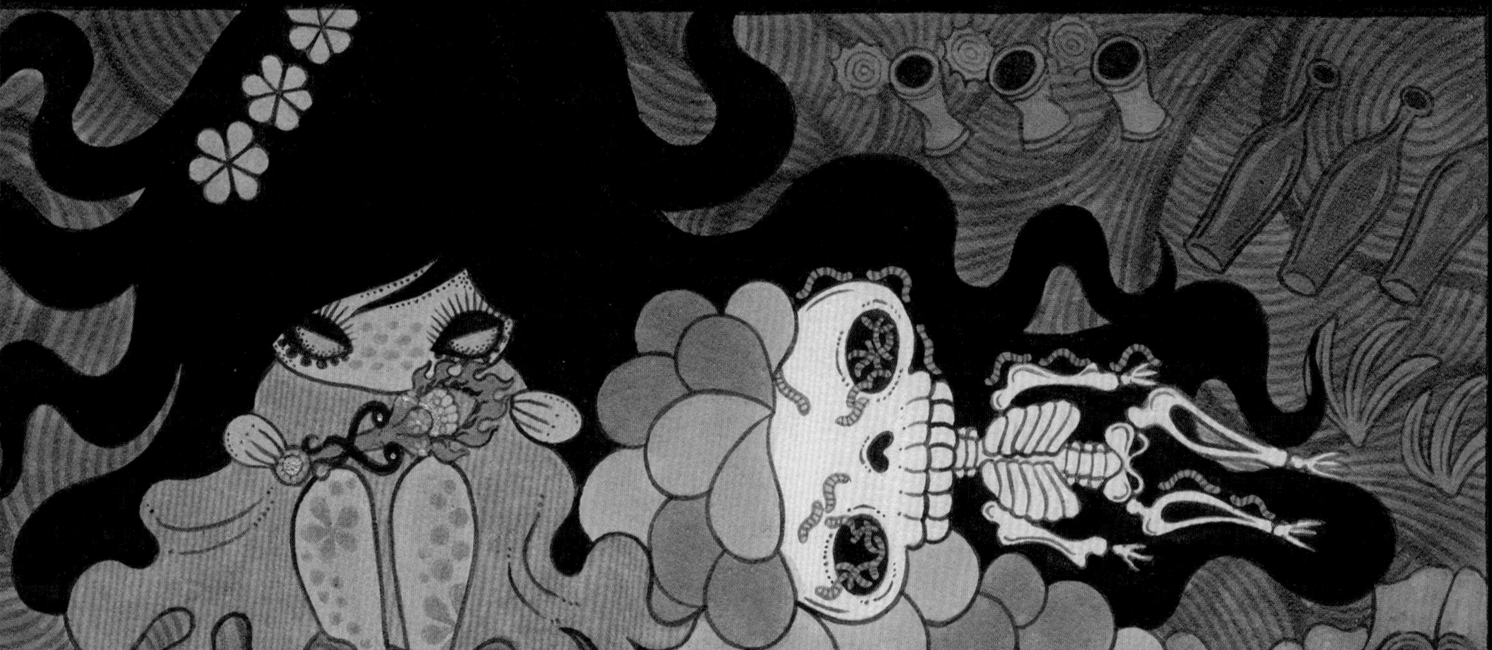

Ravina felt sad. She stayed with the old woman’s body until it turned to bones and became part of the dump.

Even though Ravina didn’t understand what the old woman had said, she began to idolize her. And even though she didn’t know how to use the wand, it became Ravina’s most beloved treasure in the entire dump.

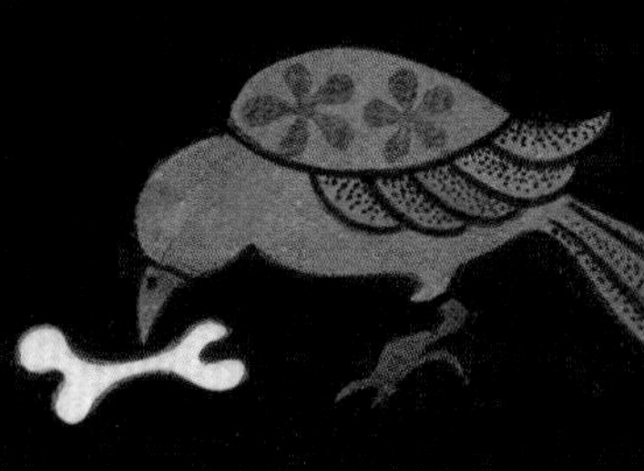

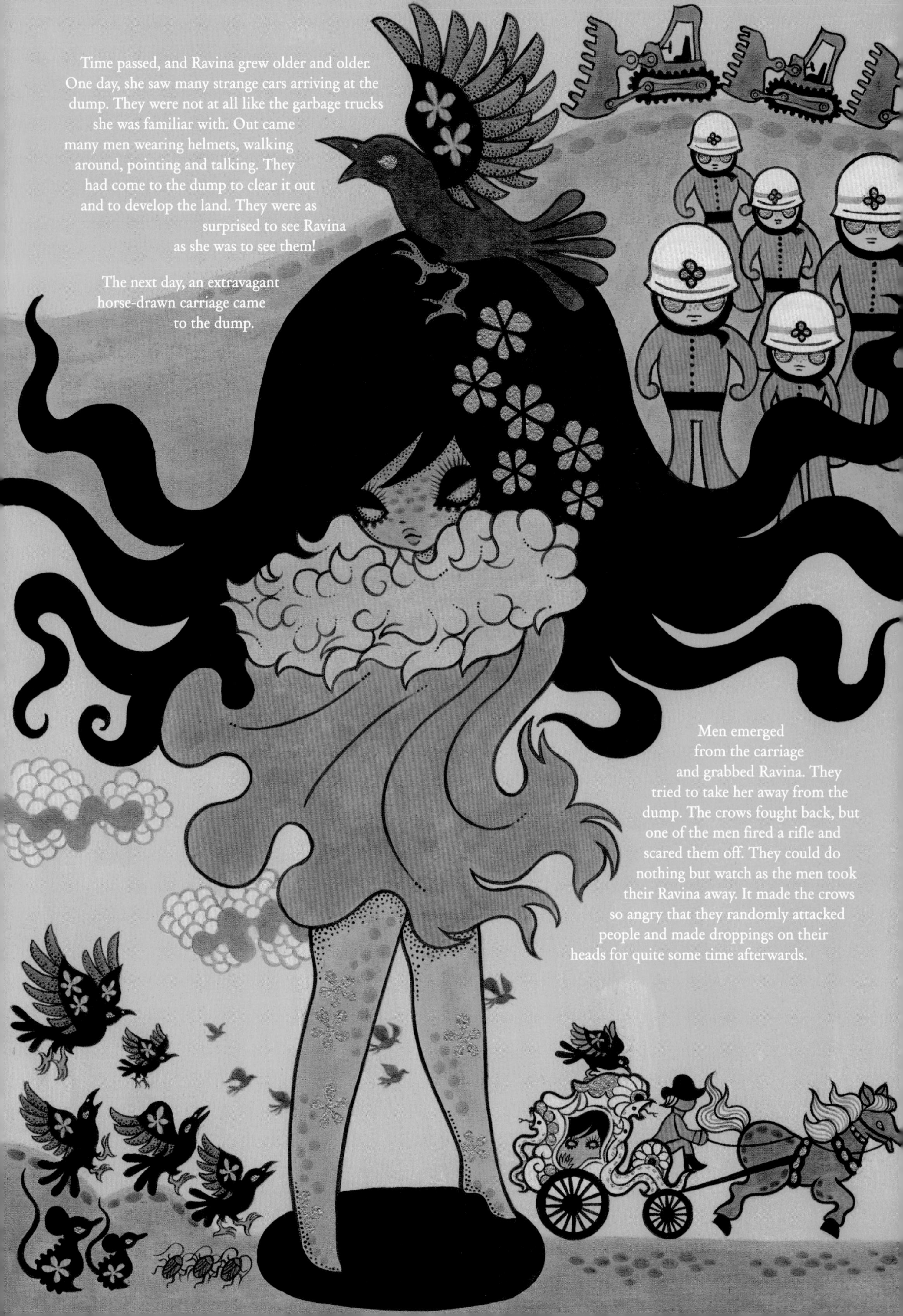

Time passed, and Ravina grew older and older. One day, she saw many strange cars arriving at the dump. They were not at all like the garbage trucks she was familiar with. Out came many men wearing helmets, walking around, pointing and talking. They had come to the dump to clear it out and to develop the land. They were as surprised to see Ravina as she was to see them!

The next day, an extravagant horse-drawn carriage came to the dump.

Men emerged from the carriage and grabbed Ravina. They tried to take her away from the dump. The crows fought back, but one of the men fired a rifle and scared them off. They could do nothing but watch as the men took their Ravina away. It made the crows so angry that they randomly attacked people and made droppings on their heads for quite some time afterwards.

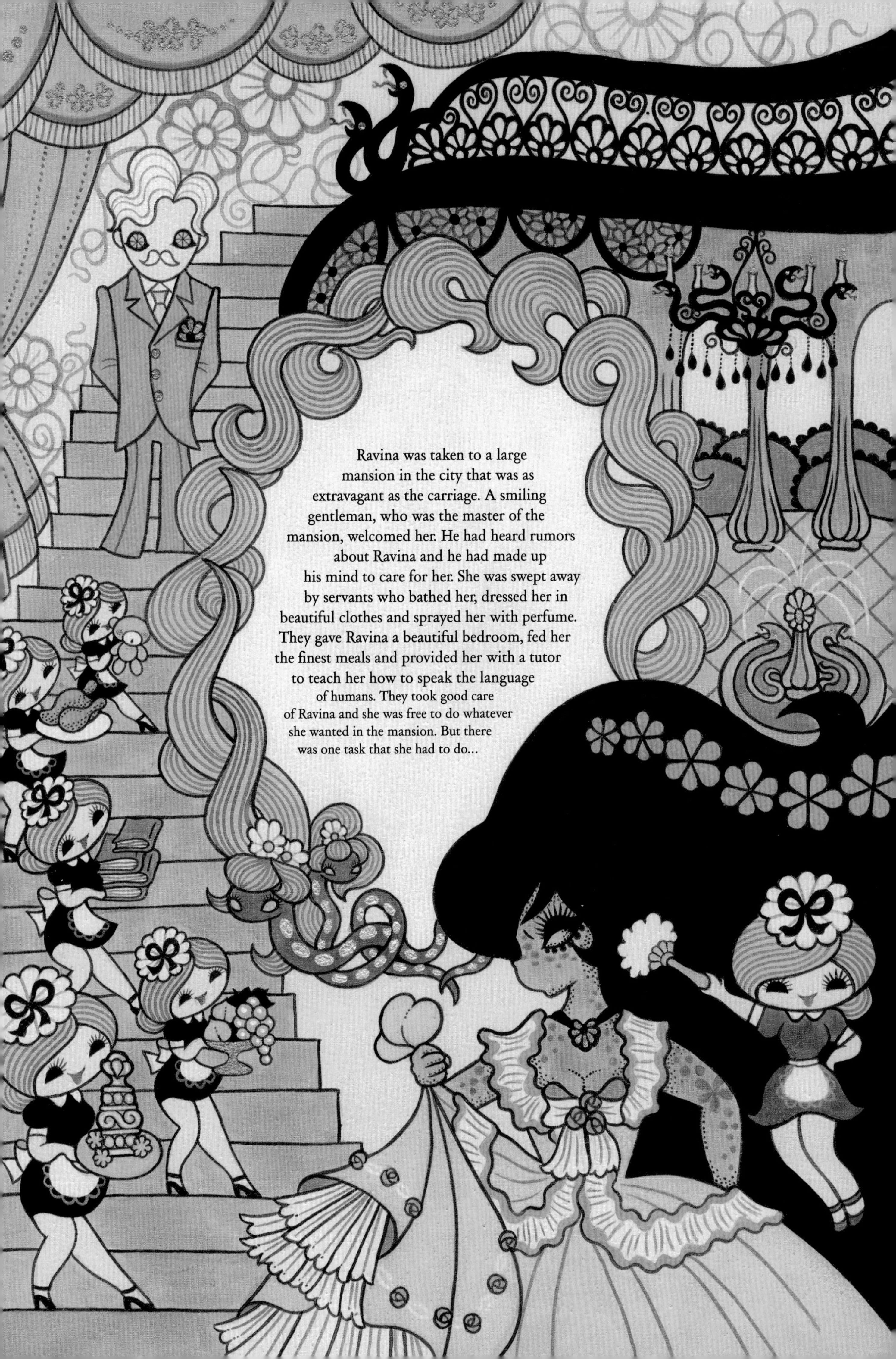

Ravina was taken to a large mansion in the city that was as extravagant as the carriage. A smiling gentleman, who was the master of the mansion, welcomed her. He had heard rumors about Ravina and he had made up his mind to care for her. She was swept away by servants who bathed her, dressed her in beautiful clothes and sprayed her with perfume. They gave Ravina a beautiful bedroom, fed her the finest meals and provided her with a tutor to teach her how to speak the language of humans. They took good care of Ravina and she was free to do whatever she wanted in the mansion. But there was one task that she had to do...

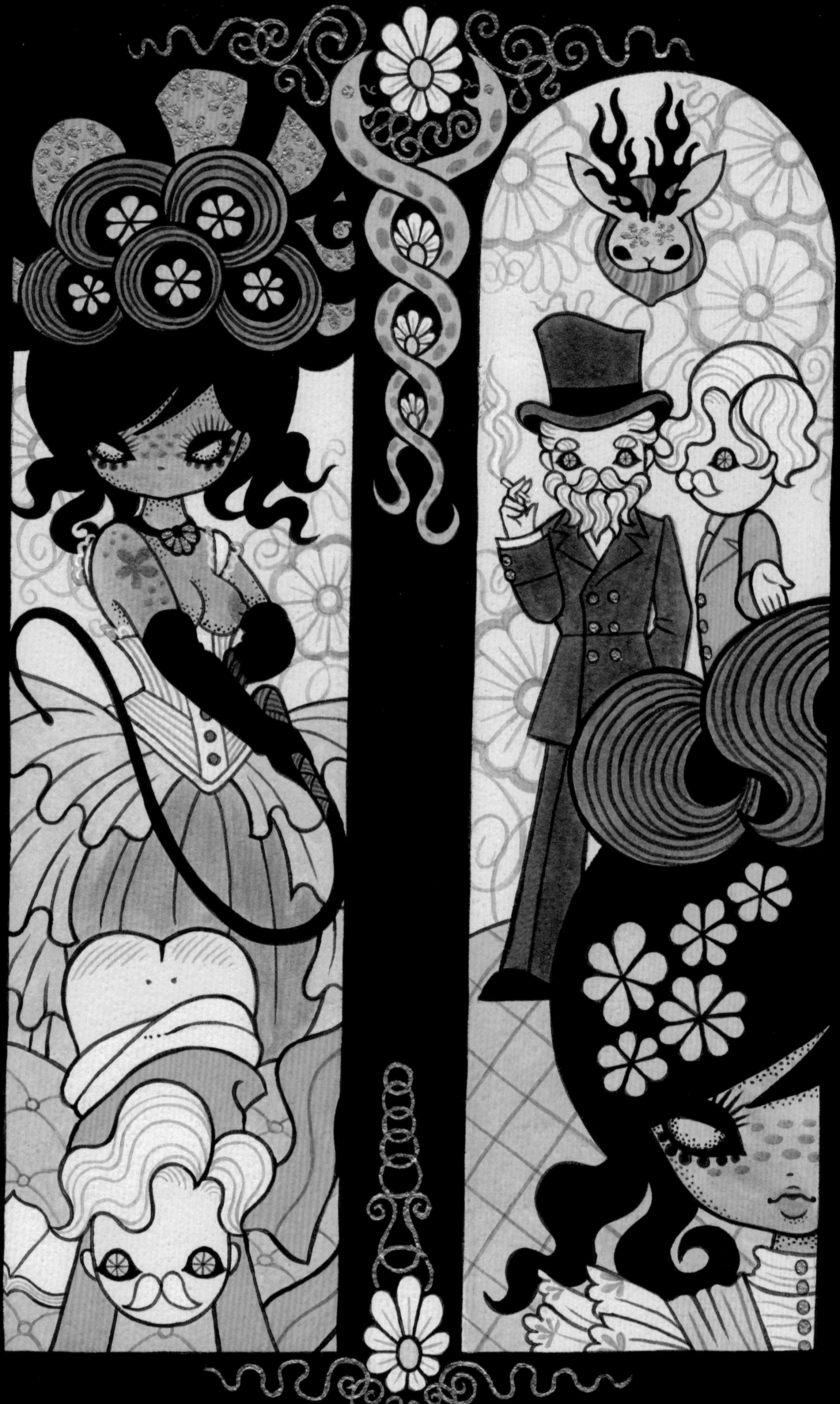

...whipping the gentleman's behind every day! She had no idea why he wanted her to do it. But it wasn't hard work and he looked very happy when she whipped him, so it didn't bother her very much.

As Ravina's whipping skills improved, the gentleman began to invite his friends to his mansion to try it out for themselves. Soon, the word spread as his friends invited their friends, and so on, and so on, until much of Ravina's time was spent whipping behinds.

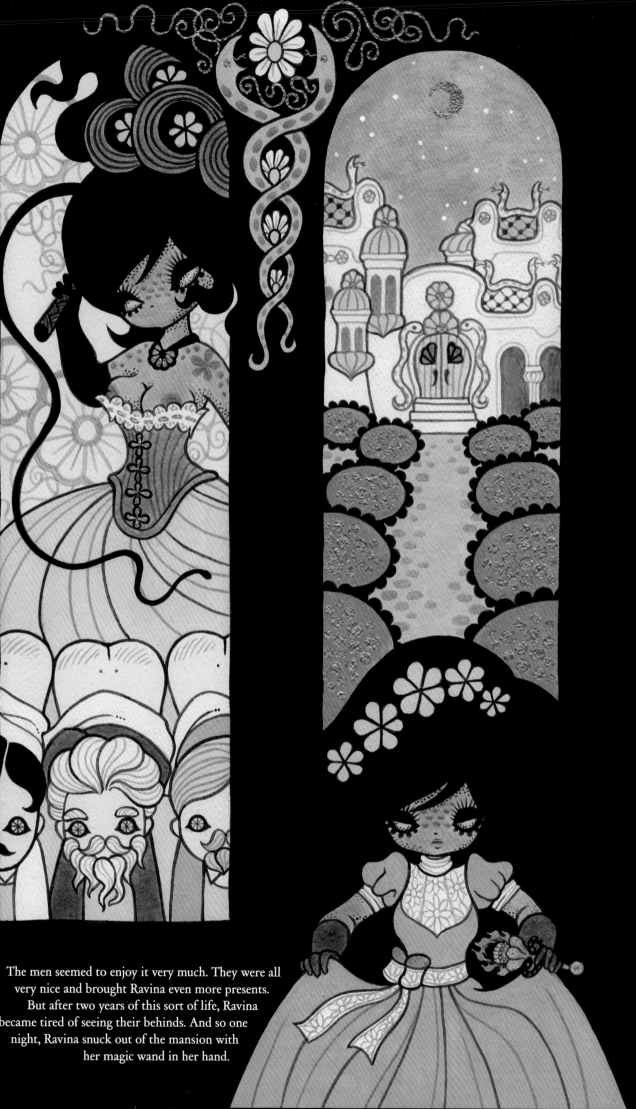

The men seemed to enjoy it very much. They were all
very nice and brought Ravina even more presents.
But after two years of this sort of life, Ravina
became tired of seeing their behinds. And so one
night, Ravina snuck out of the mansion with
her magic wand in her hand.

Ravina was careful to stay out of sight away from the gentleman and his friends. She kept to the shadows and to the edges of town until she found herself wandering into a dark forest.

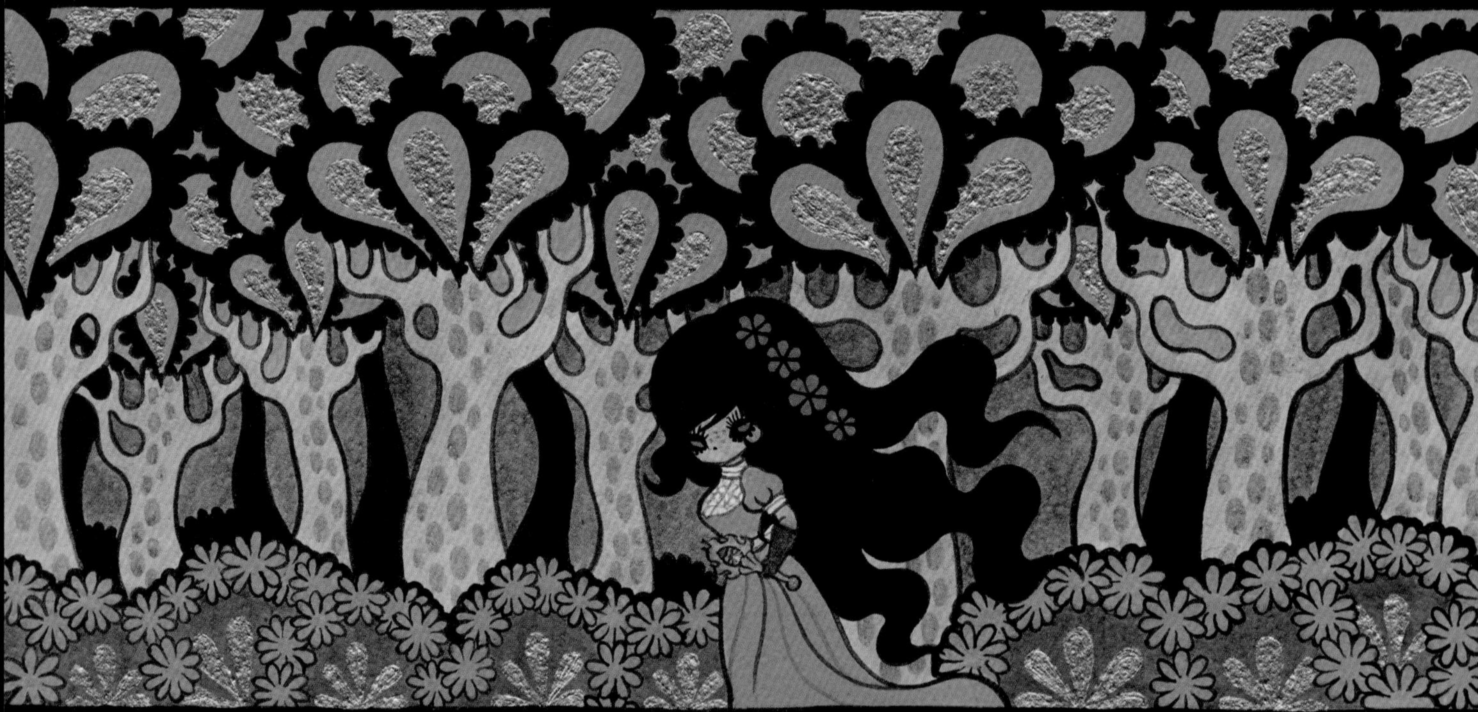

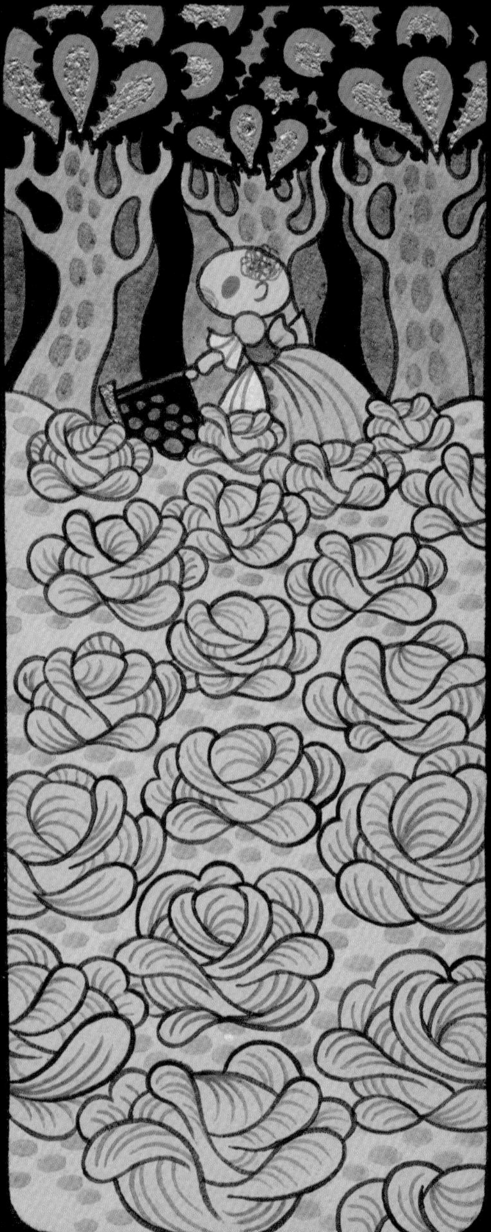

Exploring further into the woods, she came upon a small cabbage patch. There, in the middle of the patch, stood a man.

He was swinging a gardening hoe with all of his might while wearing a pretty dress.

Before Ravina could get close enough to ask the man where she was, she became dizzy from the powerful smell of the perfume he was wearing. She fell to the ground unconscious.

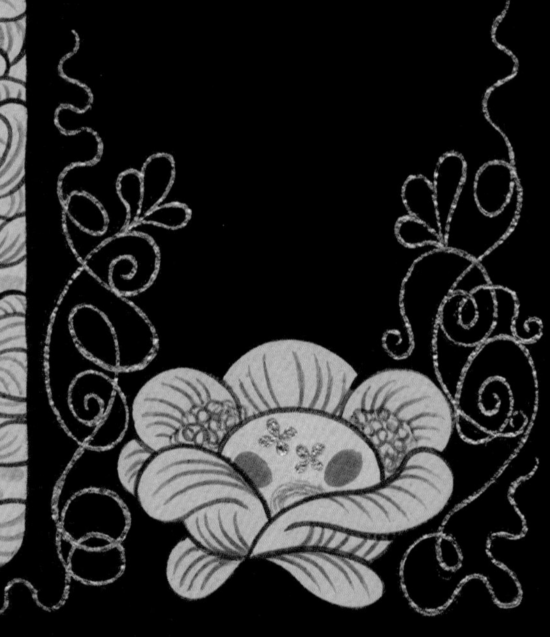

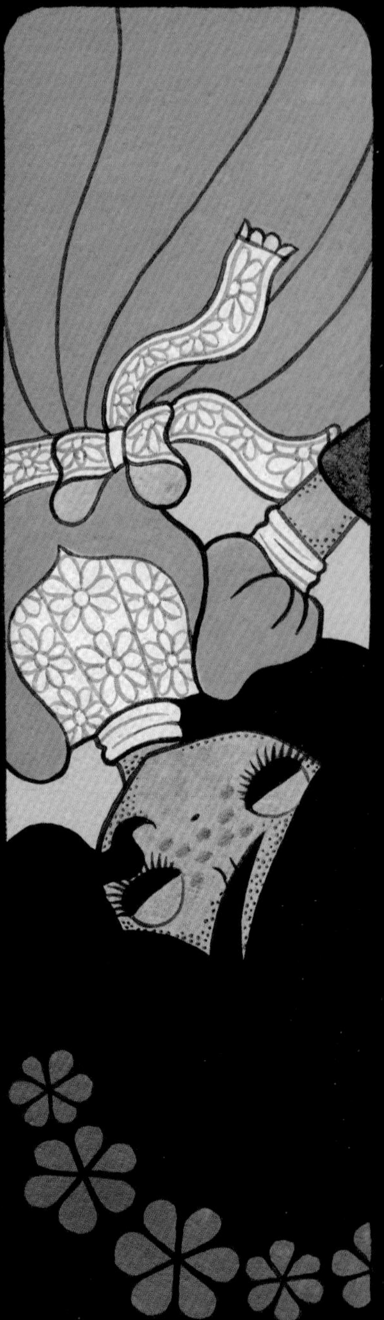

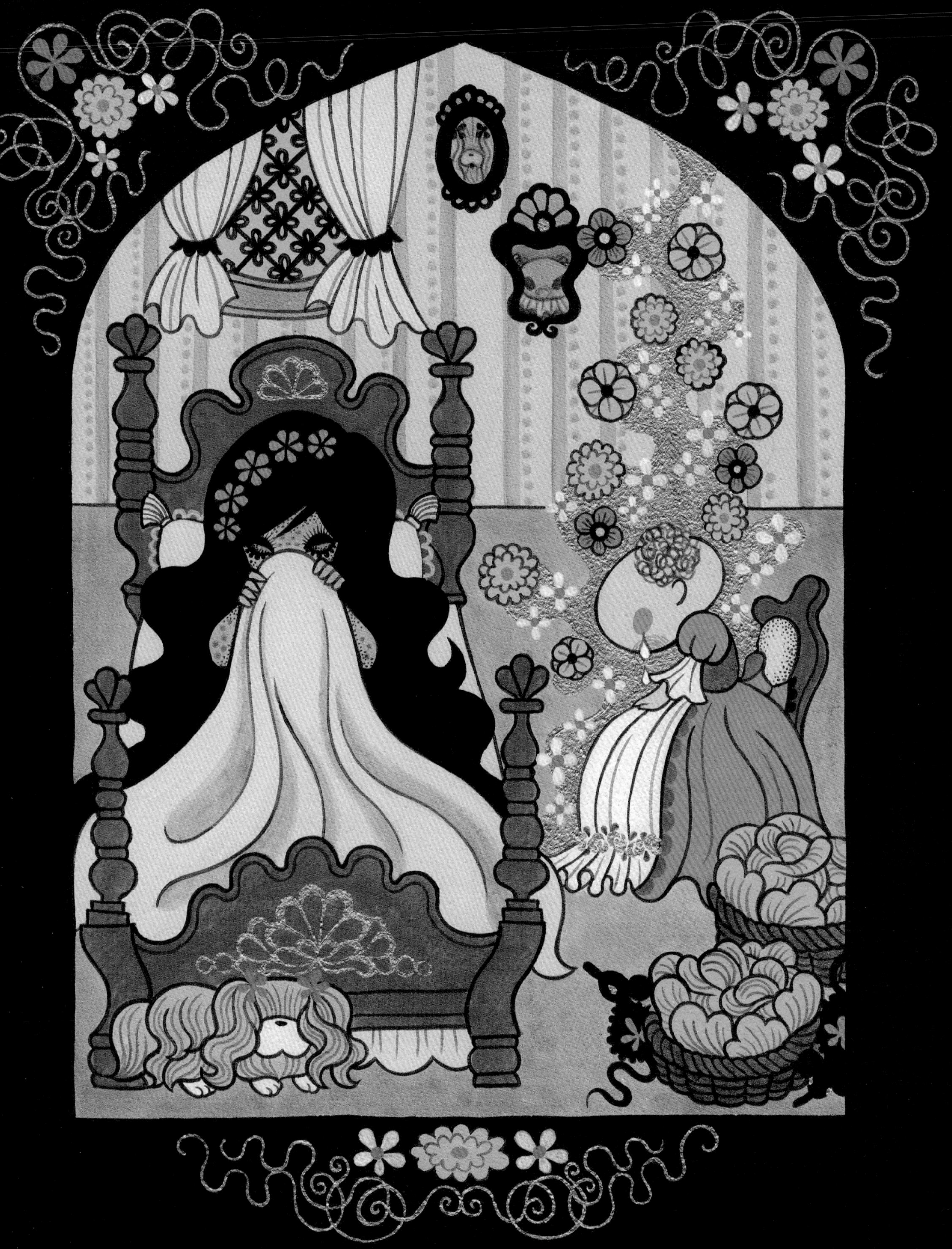

When she awoke, Ravina found herself inside a small cottage. She was in a bed with the man by her side. He looked down and said guiltily, "I know it's strange for a man to wear a dress like this… I'm sorry to have surprised you so much… But…. I LOVE pretty dresses!" Ravina quickly covered her face with the blanket. She did not want to be knocked unconscious by the smell again!

He continued sadly, "Everyone hates me because of my dresses. So I live here, alone in the forest…" Ravina said frankly from under the blanket, "I don't think it's your dresses. Rather, I think it's because you put on too much perfume."

The man blushed and exclaimed, "Why didn't anyone ever tell me before!" He ran and jumped into the river nearby and scrubbed his body hard.

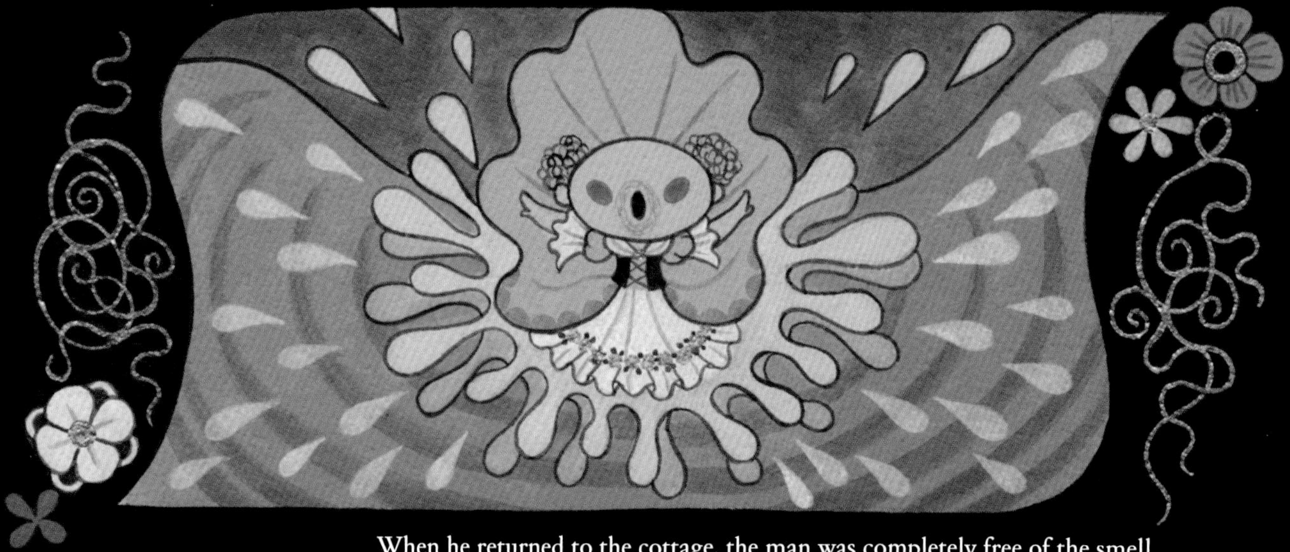

When he returned to the cottage, the man was completely free of the smell.

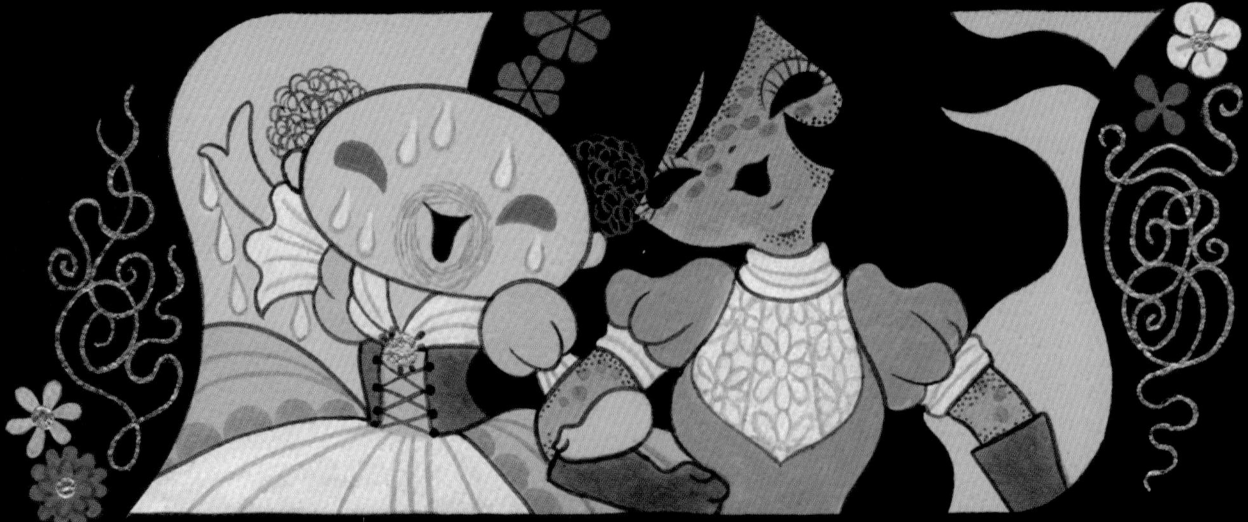

Ravina could finally breathe the same air he breathed. He was so grateful for the advice Ravina had given him that he decided to share his very best bottles of wine with her.

The man took Ravina to his favorite place. It was filled with colorful mushrooms and soft moss covering the ground. There they sat for a picnic. So happy was the man to have his first friend that they spoke and drank for hours.

Ravina was happy to have her first taste of wine and discovered that she liked it a lot. The man was impressed by the way she kept swilling from the bottles.

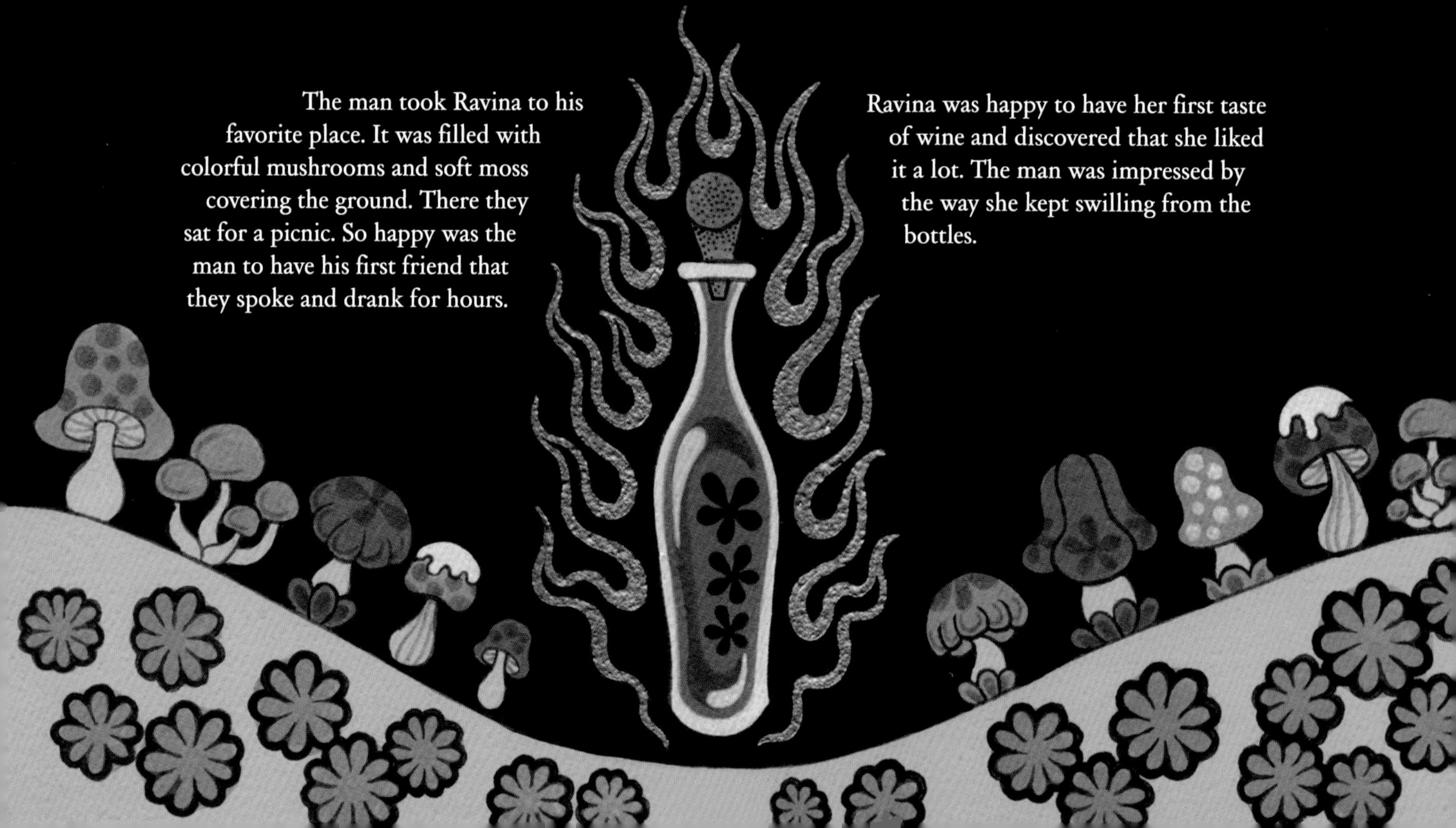

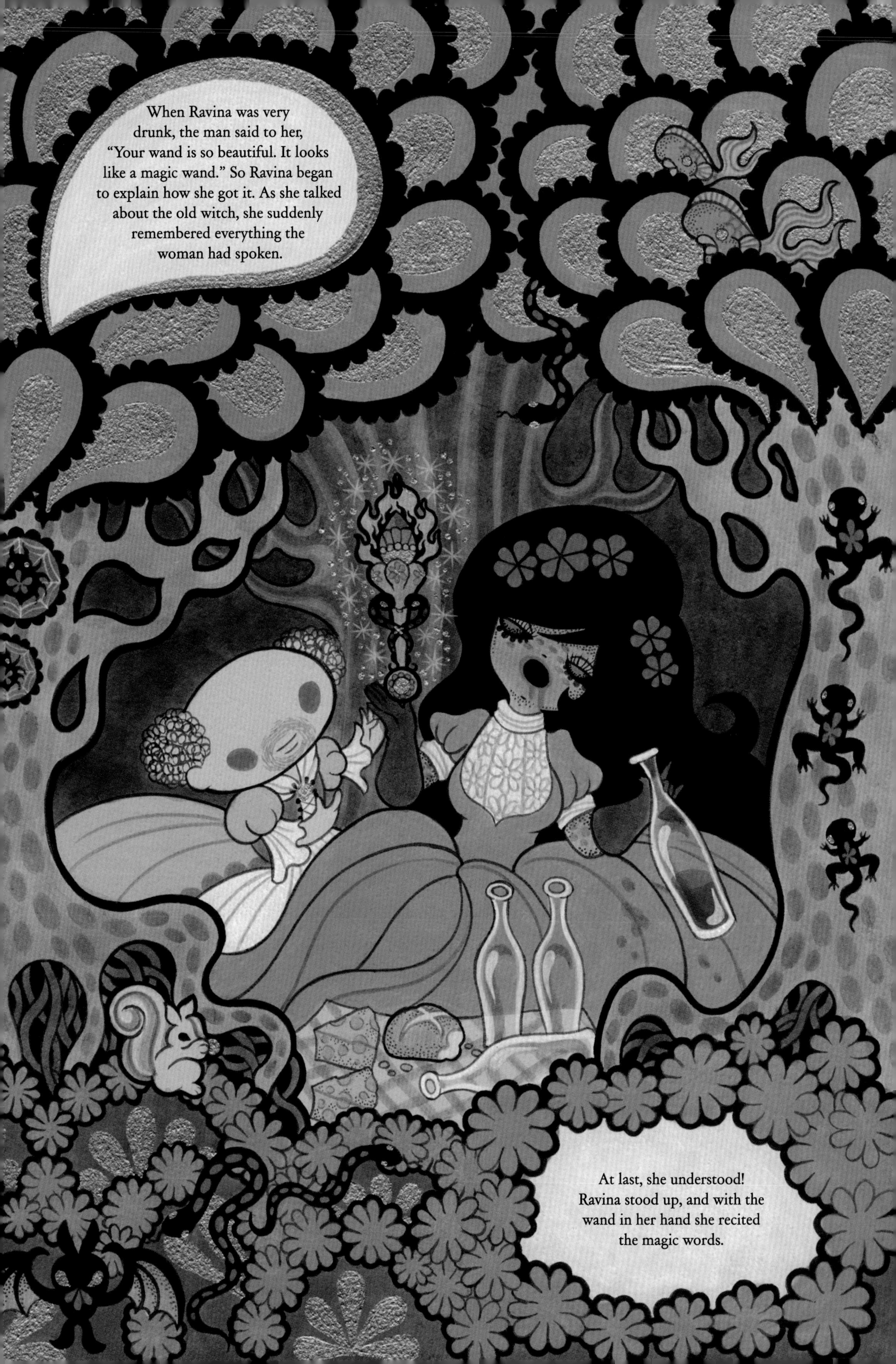
When Ravina was very drunk, the man said to her, "Your wand is so beautiful. It looks like a magic wand." So Ravina began to explain how she got it. As she talked about the old witch, she suddenly remembered everything the woman had spoken.
At last, she understood! Ravina stood up, and with the wand in her hand she recited the magic words.

To her amazement, and to the man's delight, something wonderful happened. The spell that Ravina cast caused all of the colorful mushrooms around them to dance as she waved the wand! Ravina and the man danced all night with the mushrooms until dawn.

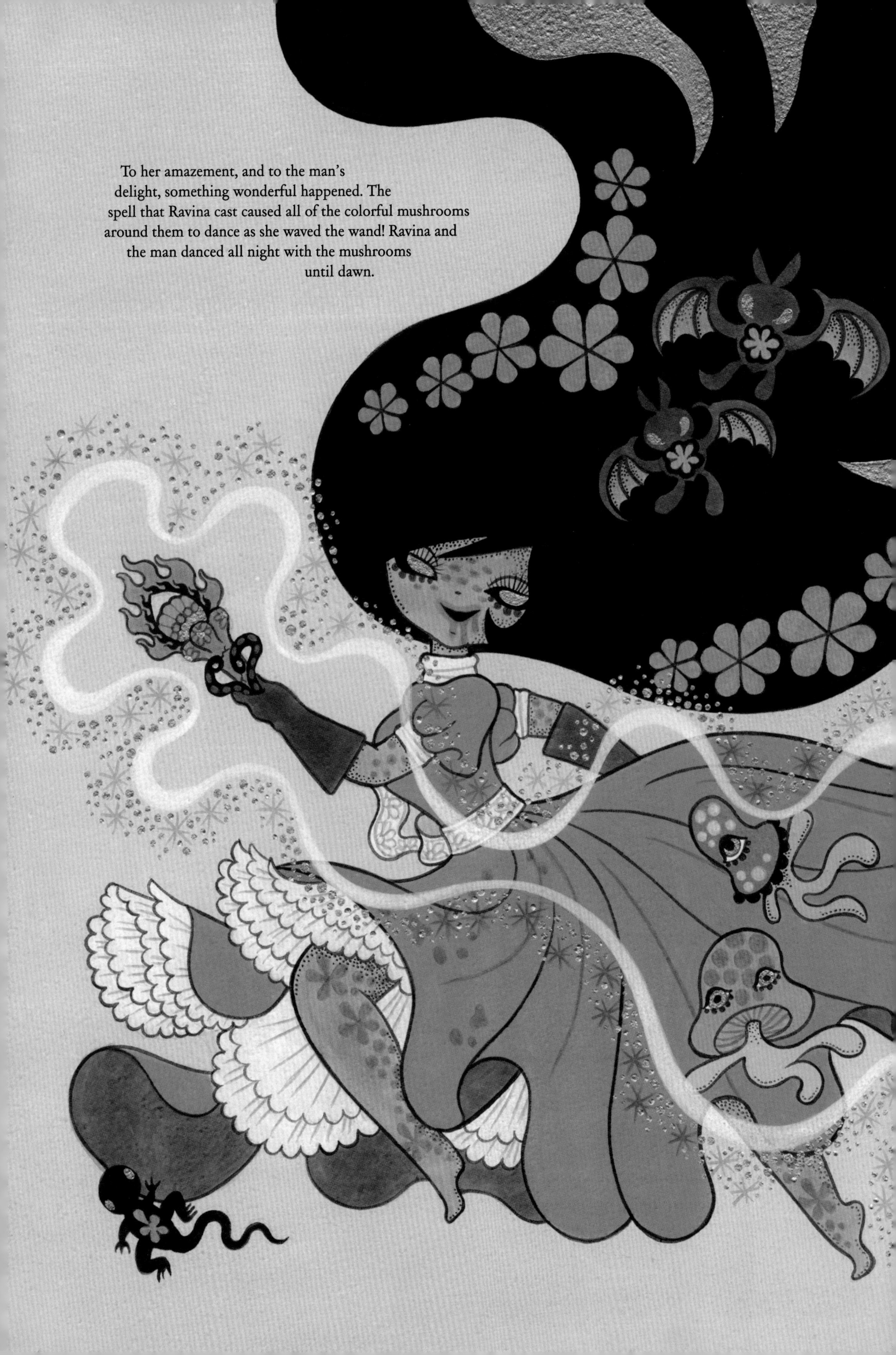

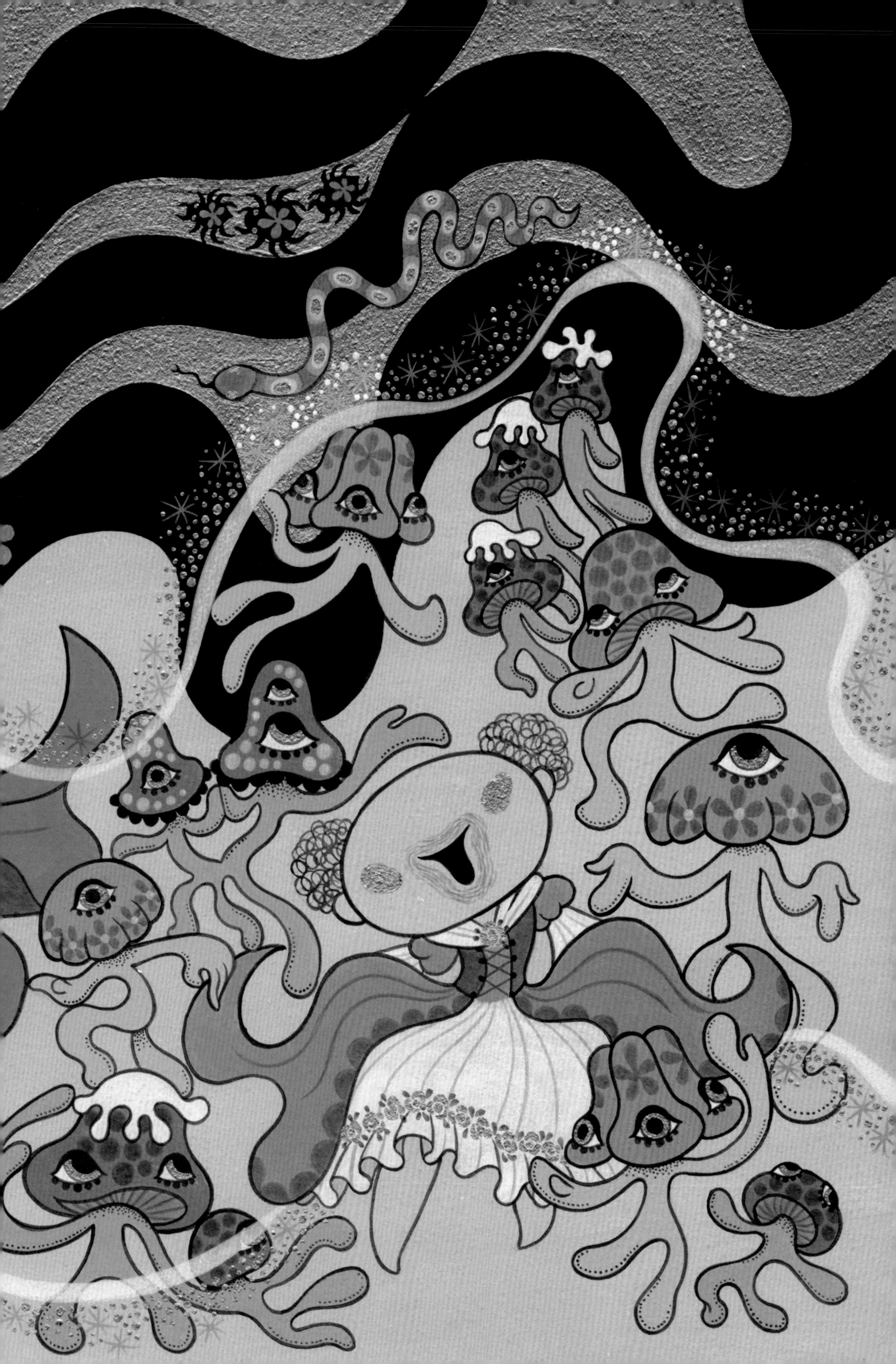

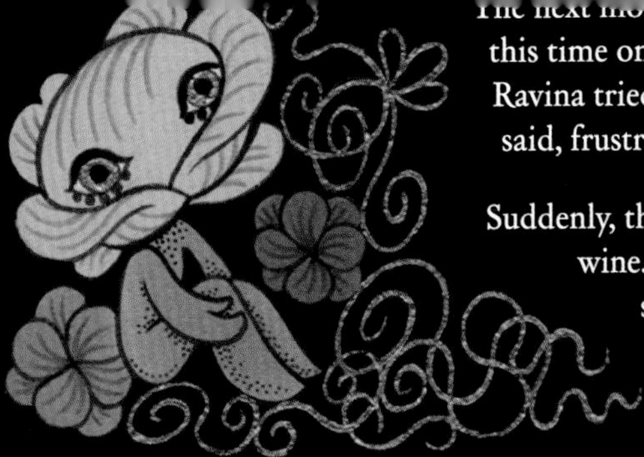

The next morning, Ravina and the man decided to go outside to try another spell, this time on the cabbages in the garden. But somehow, no matter how much Ravina tried, she couldn't come up with the right spell. "That's odd," she said, frustrated. "I was able to say it yesterday..."

Suddenly, the man had an idea. He ran inside and quickly returned with another bottle of wine. He exclaimed, "Maybe this will help!" and handed the bottle to Ravina. As she got drunk, the magic words soon began to spring naturally from her lips.

Ravina waved her wand...

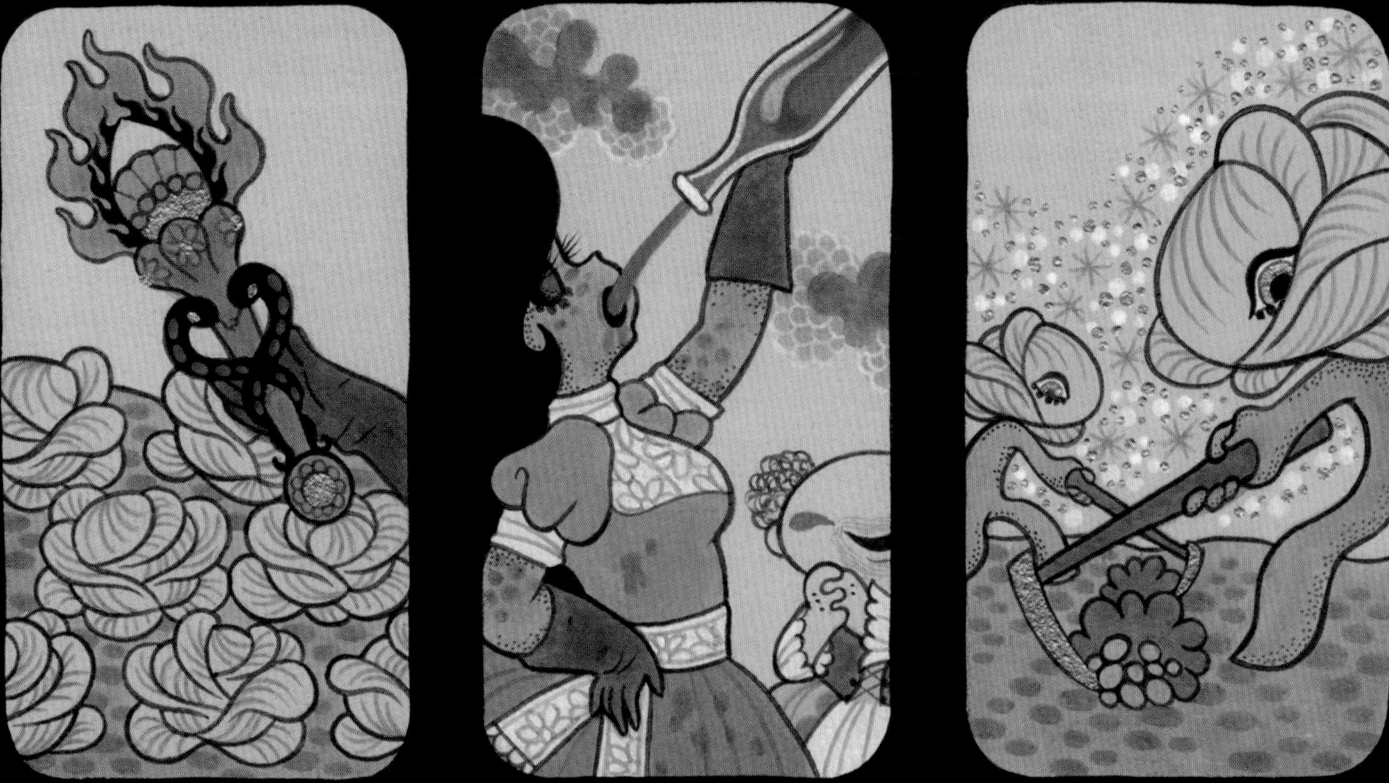

Magically, the cabbages rose up and started to work on the field! The man said, "It seems you need to be drunk to cast your spells. It's a bit inconvenient, but at least you can use your magic this way!" The man began to wonder what else Ravina could do with her wand. His mind turned to his sick grandmother, whom he had left in the village. Maybe Ravina could cure her with magic? The pair decided to leave the cottage and they went to the village with some bottles of wine in tow.

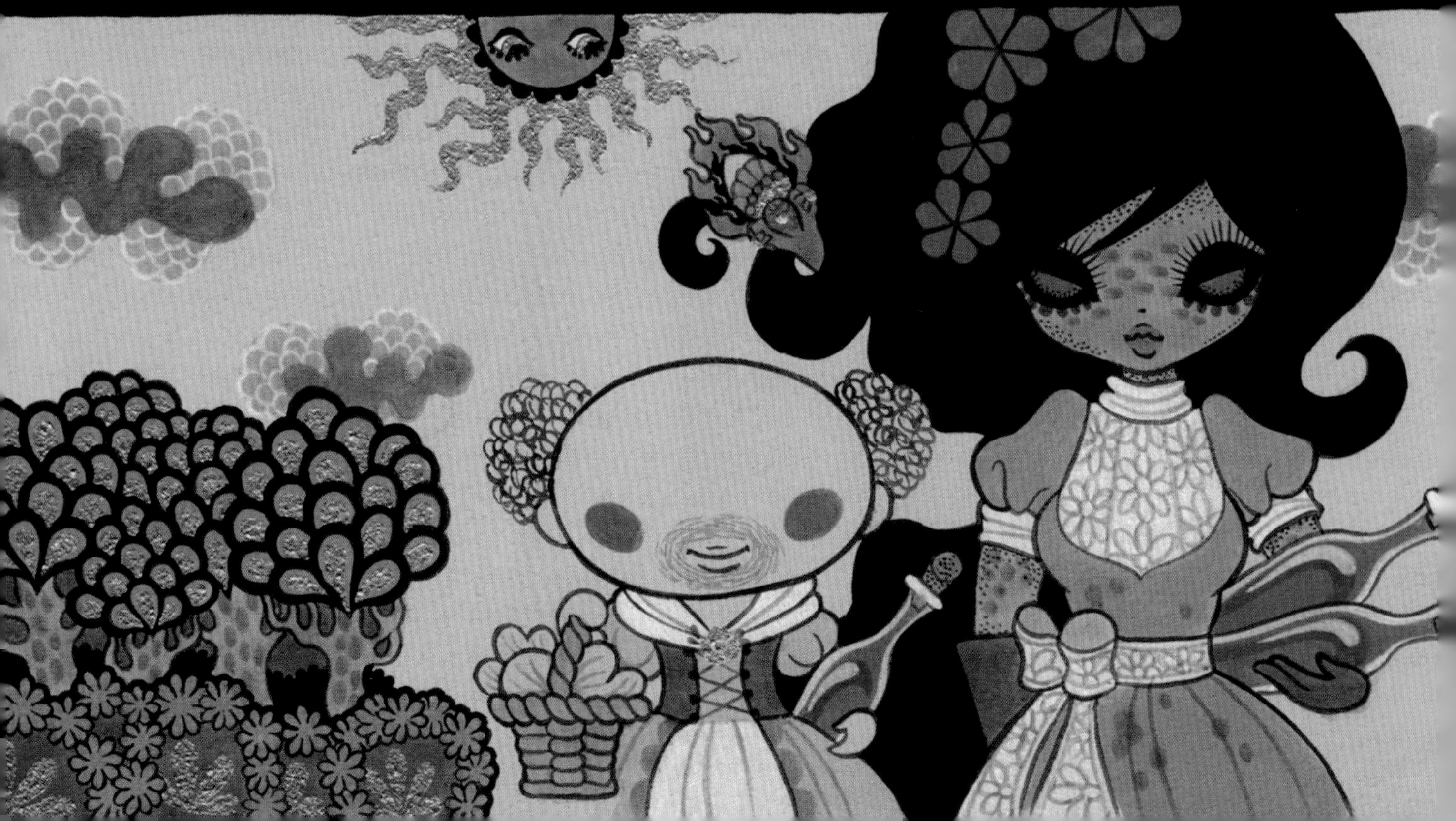

When Ravina and the man arrived at the village,
they found something very shocking. In all of the villager's yards were cows
and sheep, lying lifelessly on their backs!

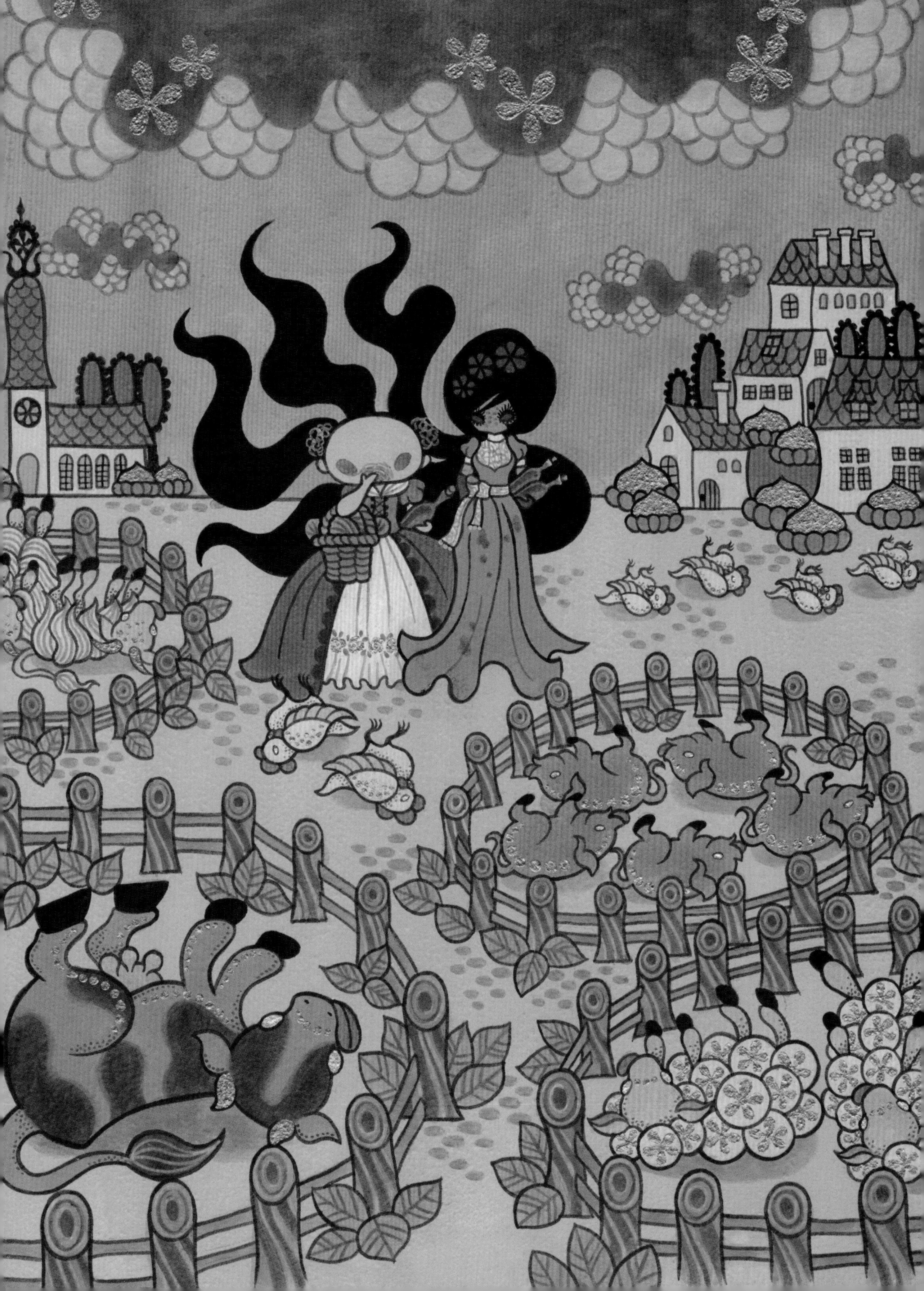

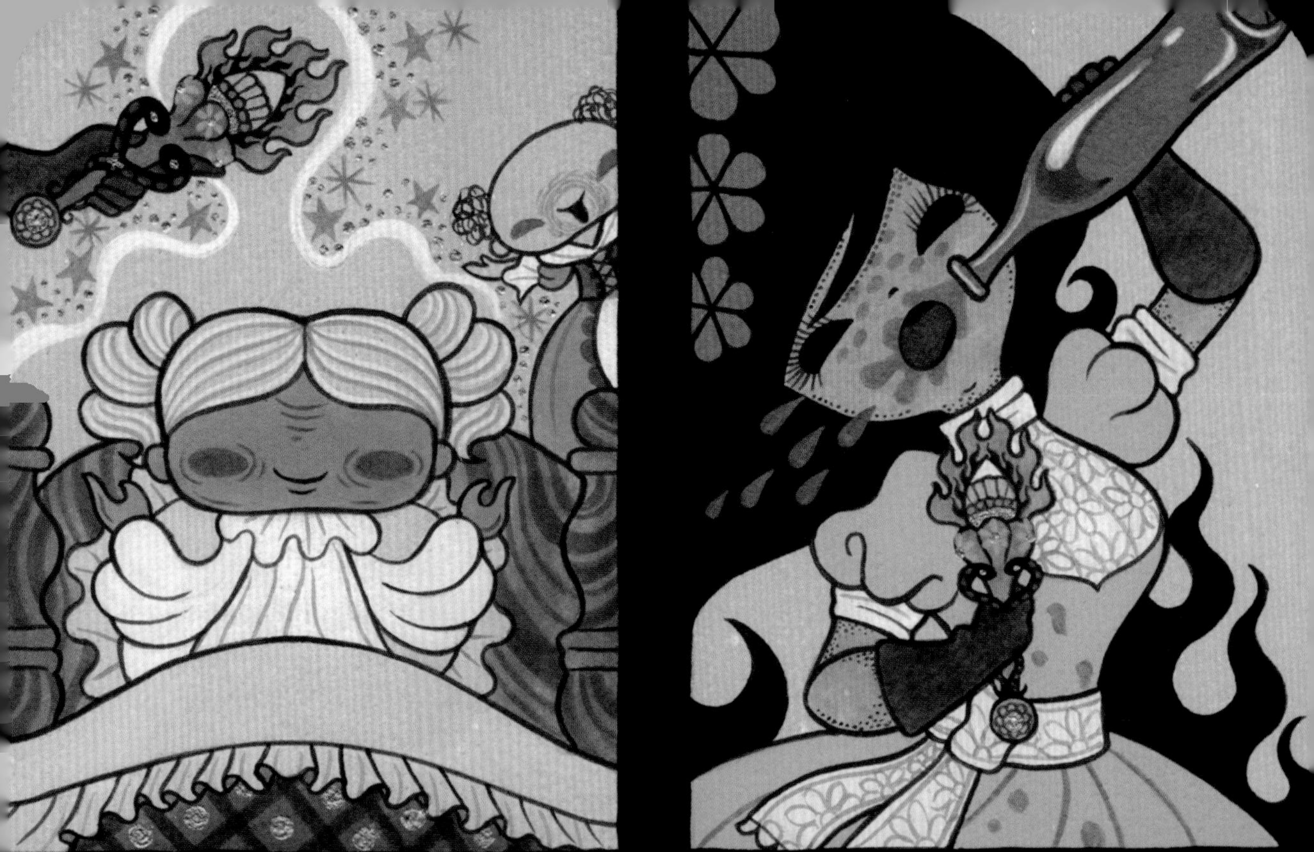

It was very easy for Ravina to cure the man's grandmother. She thanked Ravina and told them about what had happened to the animals. It seemed that a contagious disease had spread across the village that made all the animals fall ill. "Well, why not see if we can cure them, too?" suggested the man. And so he and Ravina went door to door, curing the animals one by one in exchange for a glass of wine

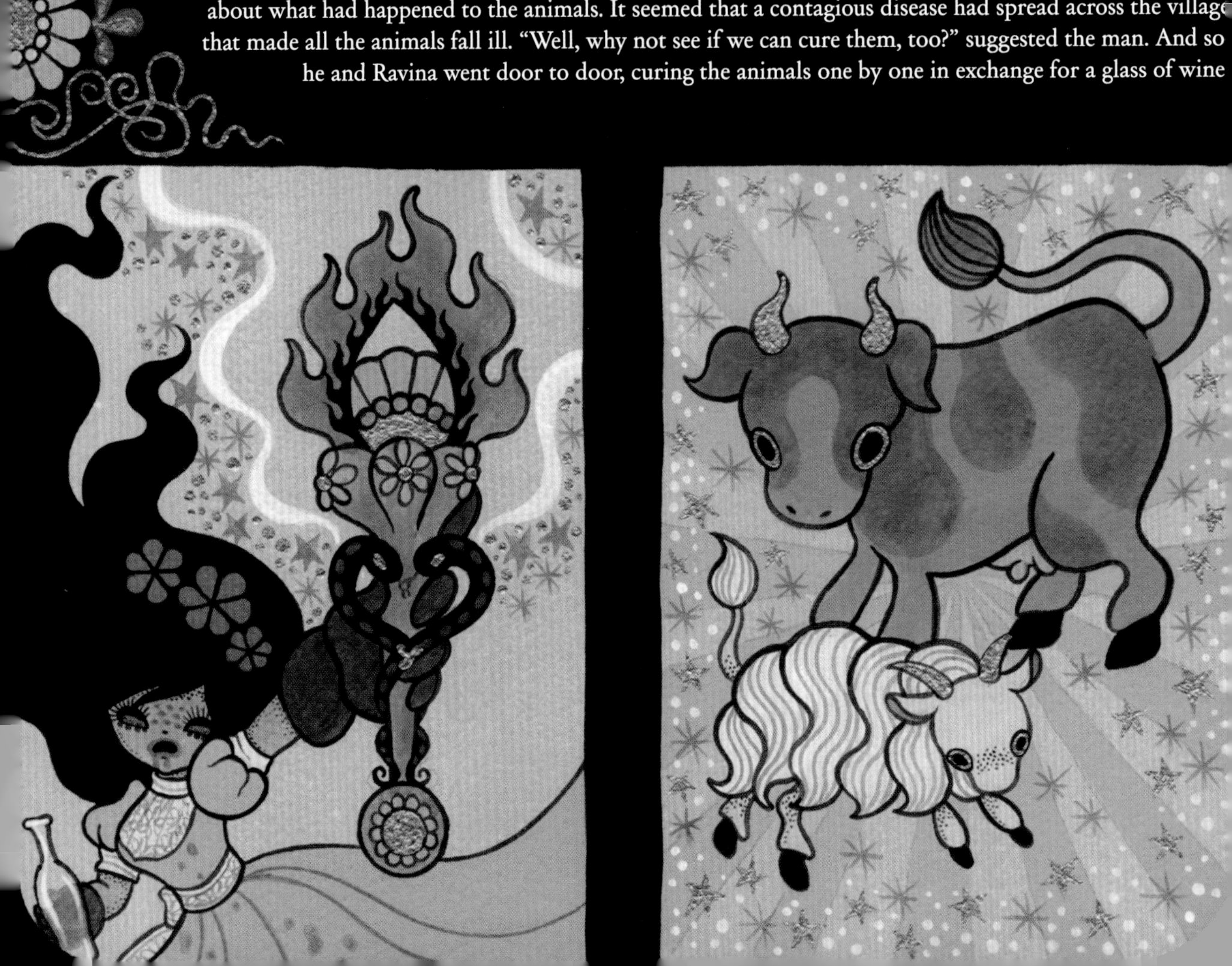

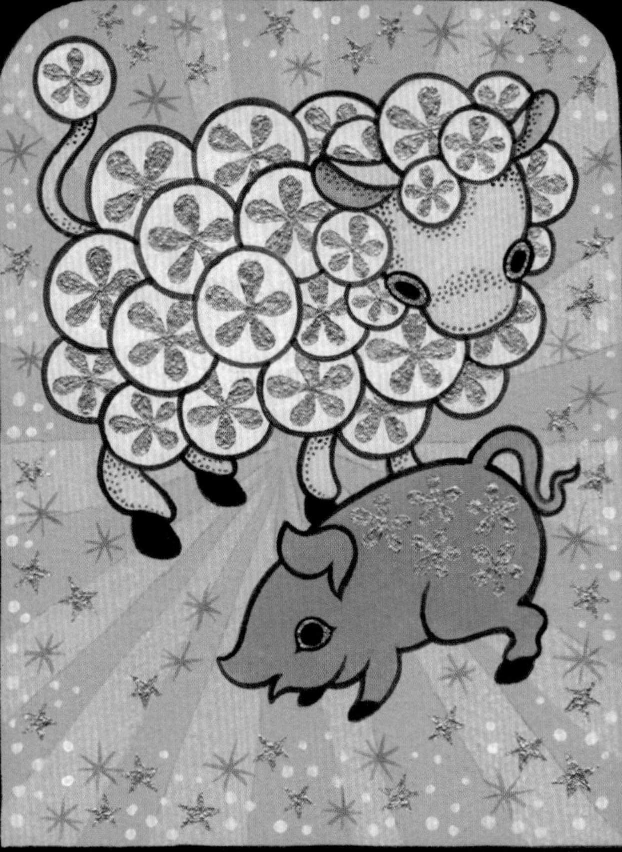

The villagers, so happy at what Ravina had done for them, decided to throw a party in her honor.

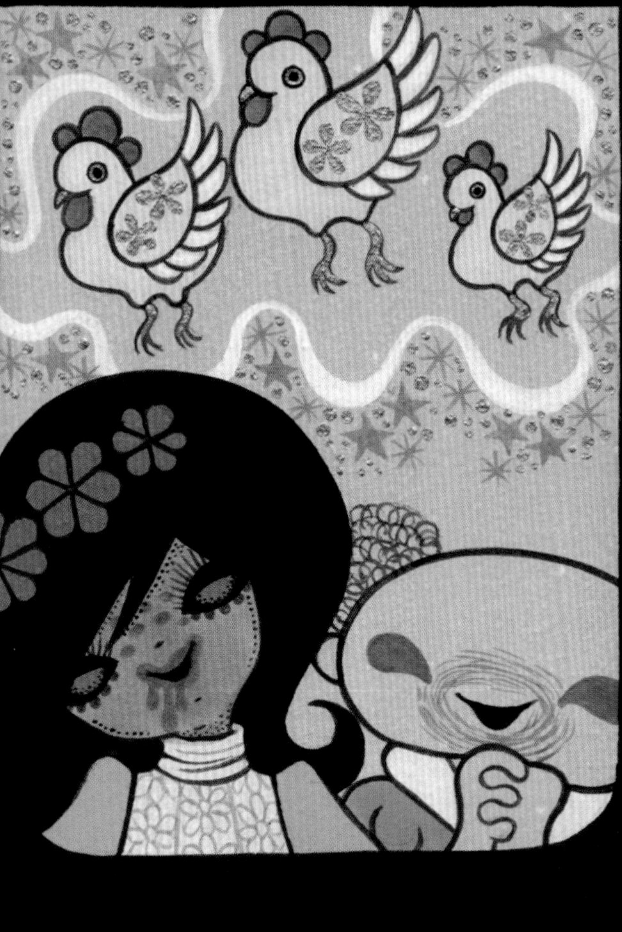

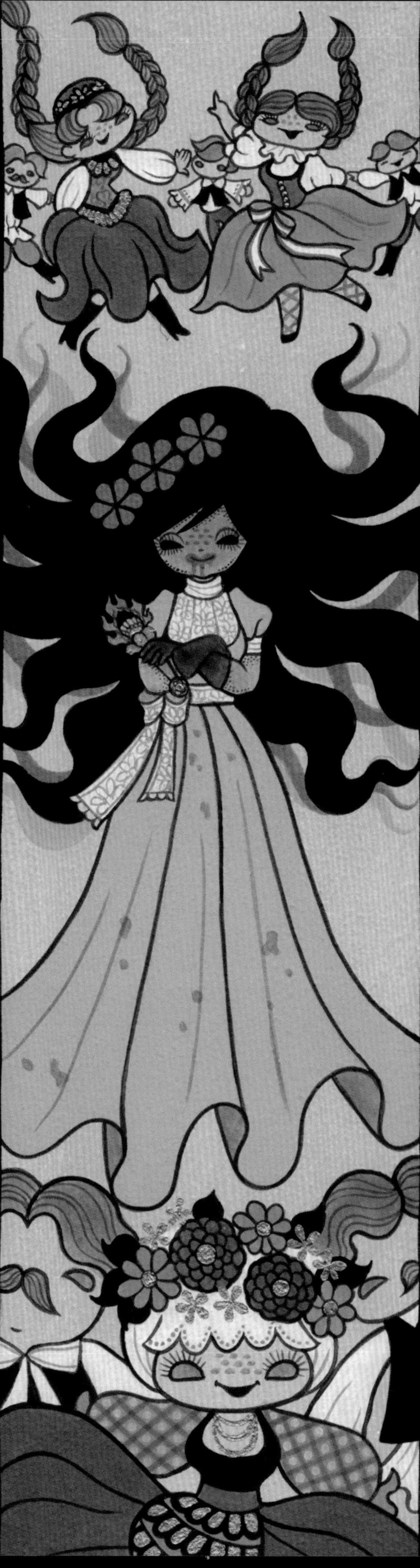

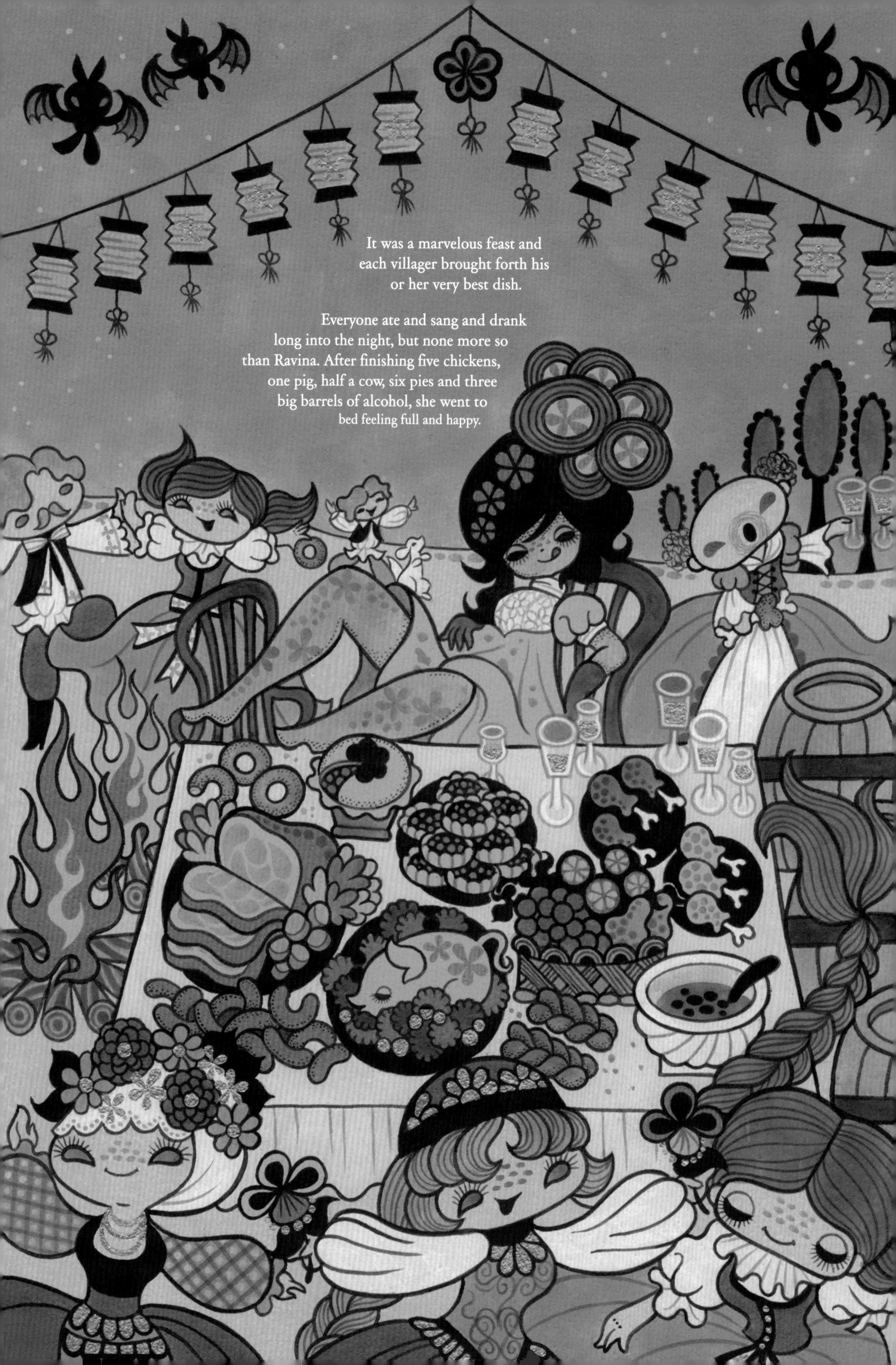

It was a marvelous feast and each villager brought forth his or her very best dish.

Everyone ate and sang and drank long into the night, but none more so than Ravina. After finishing five chickens, one pig, half a cow, six pies and three big barrels of alcohol, she went to bed feeling full and happy.

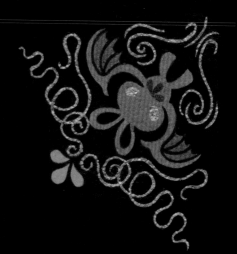

The next morning, Ravina awoke to find everyone
in the village suffering from a terrible stomach illness.
Something in the food may have been bad...

...but because she grew up in a dump,
Ravina's stomach was strong.

She could eat pretty much anything without getting sick.

But the villagers were unaware of this.
They saw that Ravina was the only one who was
up and about. They began to wonder if this girl
had used her magic to poison them. They rose
up and began to chase after her!

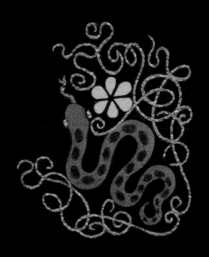

The man in the dress was the only one on Ravina's side. He snuck Ravina into his grandmother's house and said, "It's dangerous here! You must hurry up and escape! Thank you for everything! I hope to see you again one day!" He showed Ravina the safest way out of the village and she ran away.

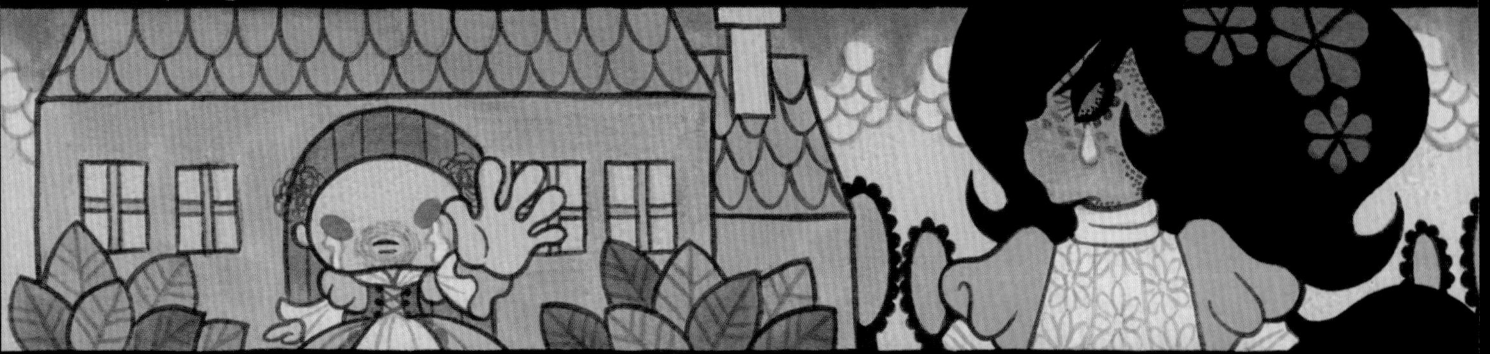

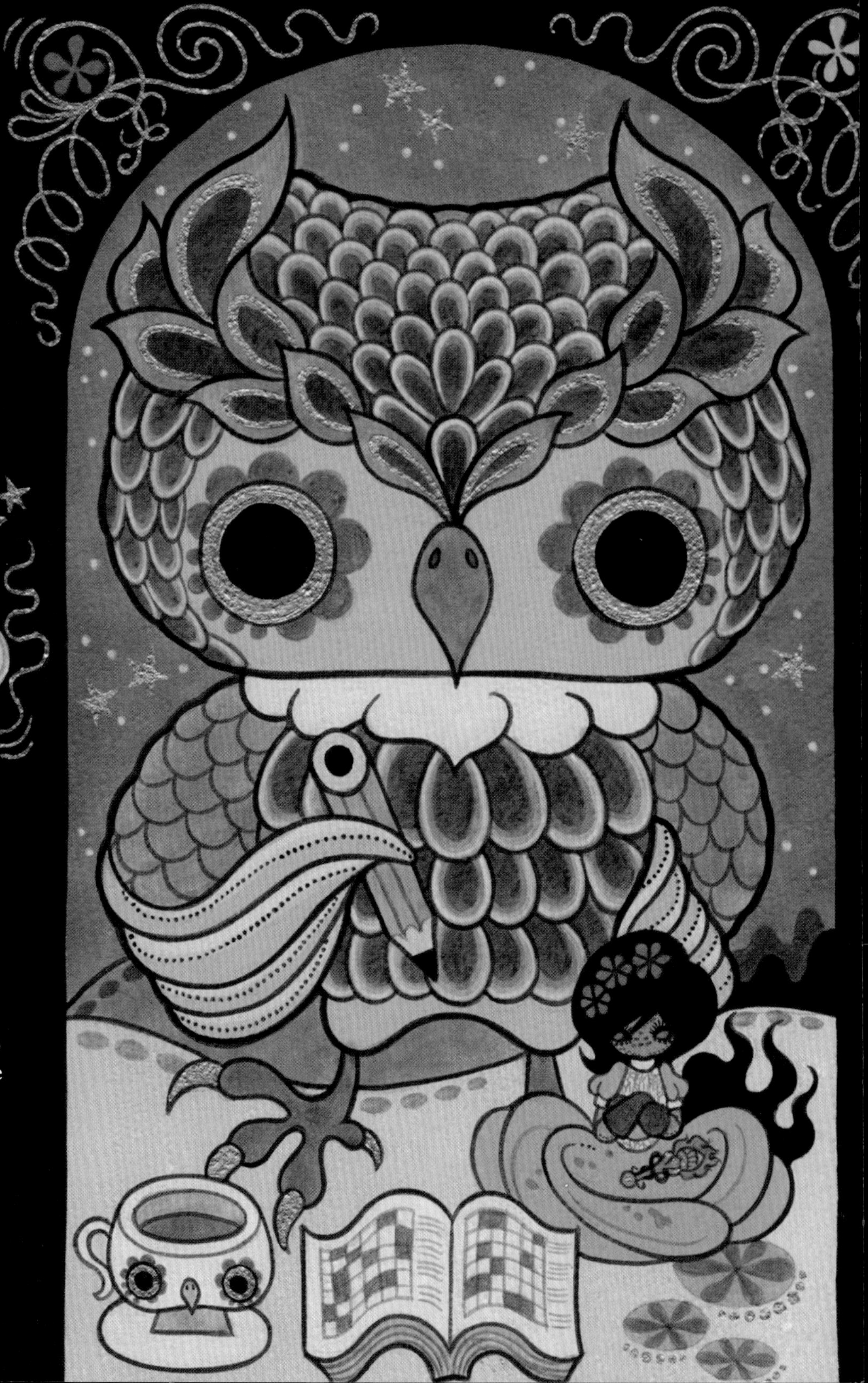

After running for a long, long time, Ravina decided to rest in a field far from the village. As she sat, thinking of what to do next, Ravina heard some muttering.

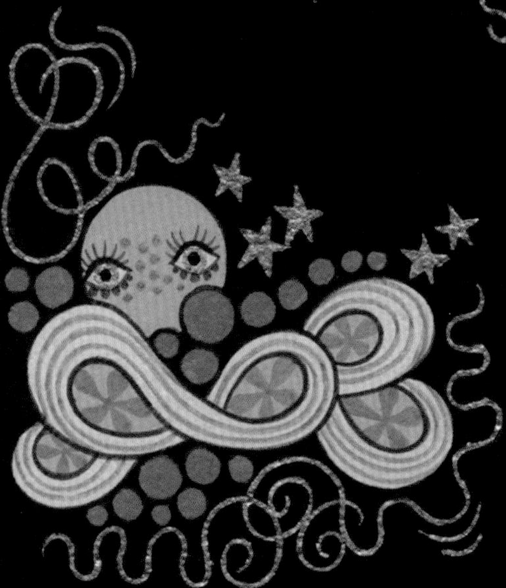

Walking closer to the noise, she saw a gigantic owl, working on a crossword puzzle.

This was the first time Ravina had ever seen such a creature. He looked a little bit like a large crow to her, so she called out to him in the language of the crows.

The owl was baffled at first, but as they continued to talk, somehow they managed to understand each other. It turned out that crow and owl language shared a lot in common.

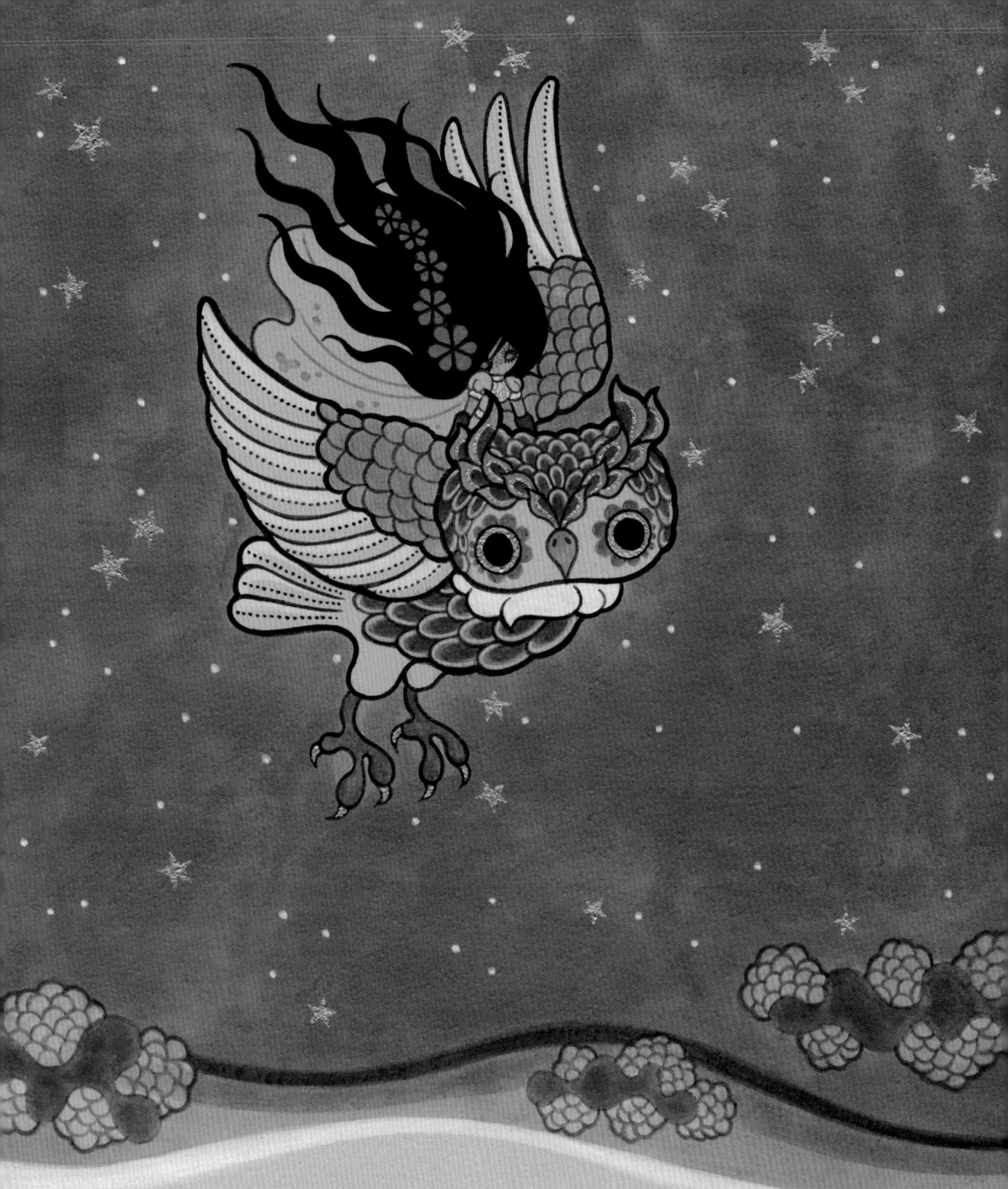

Ravina offered to help the owl to finish his crossword
if he would take her far away to where she could easily get some food.

The owl accepted the offer and the two stayed up all night.
They finished the crossword puzzle and took to the skies at dawn.

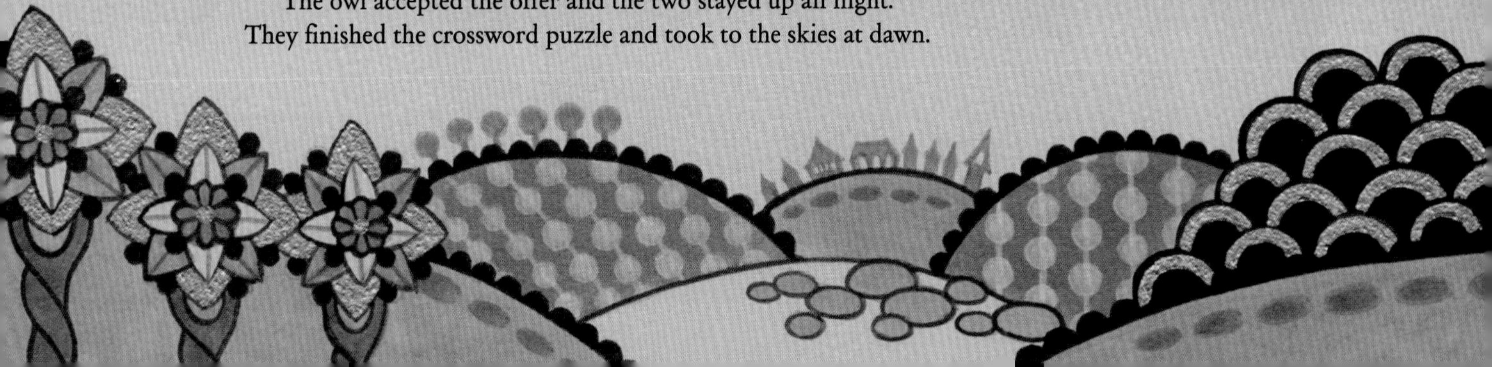

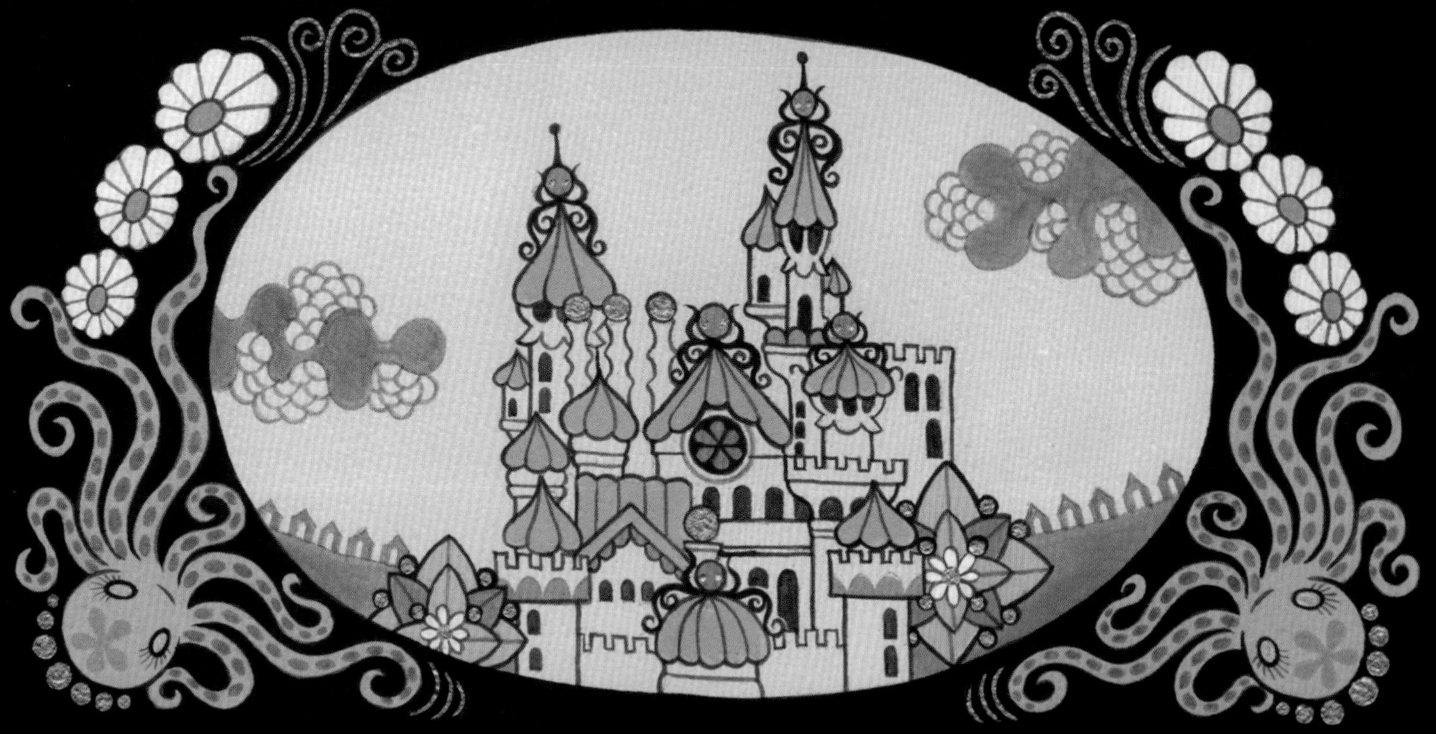

As they flew in the morning sun, they finally found a town
with a large castle in the center, surrounded by smaller houses.
"This looks like a fine place to land!" Ravina told the owl.

The people who saw the giant owl with a girl on its back landing in the center of the plaza became scared and ran away. Ravina said thank you and goodbye to the owl.

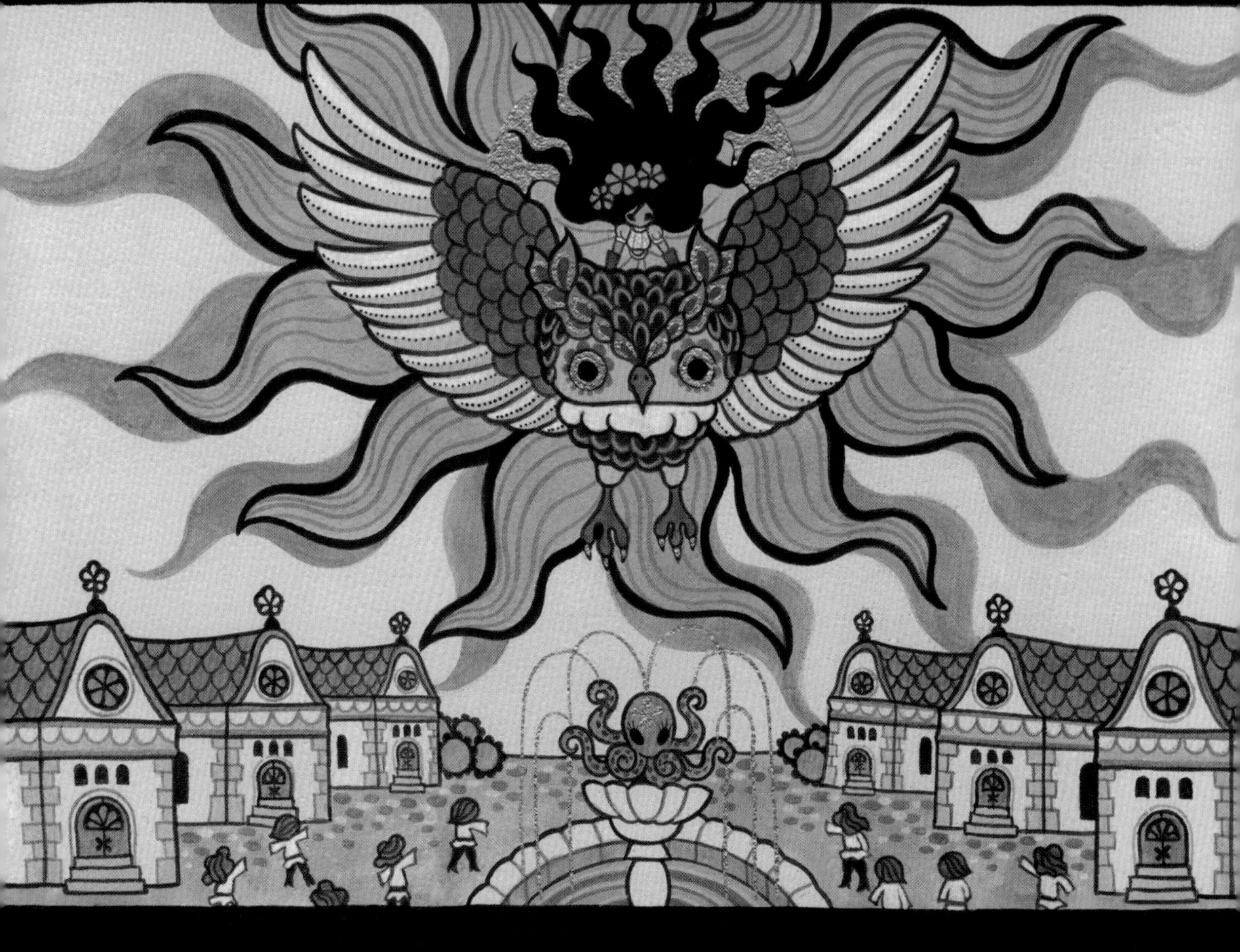

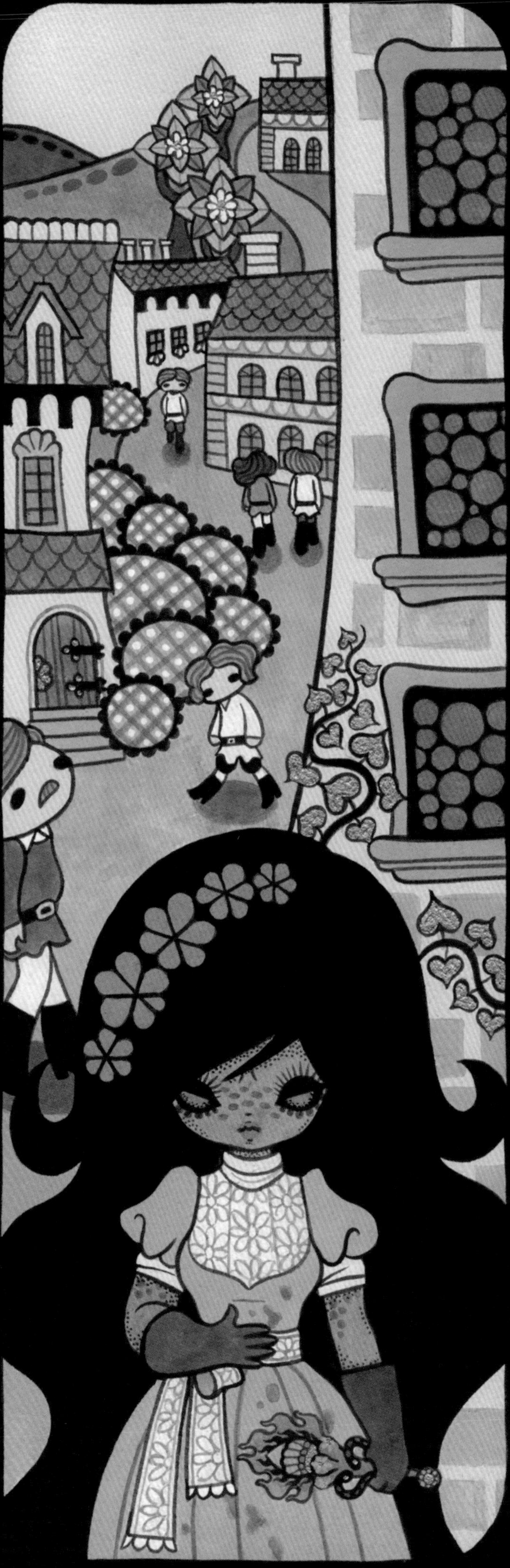

Alone once more, Ravina soon realized she was very hungry. She went from house to house, seeing if anyone had any food they could spare, but everyone said they had nothing to eat.

Noticing that the people all seemed depressed in this town, Ravina realized that everyone who lived there was a man. "Why are there no woman here?" she wondered.

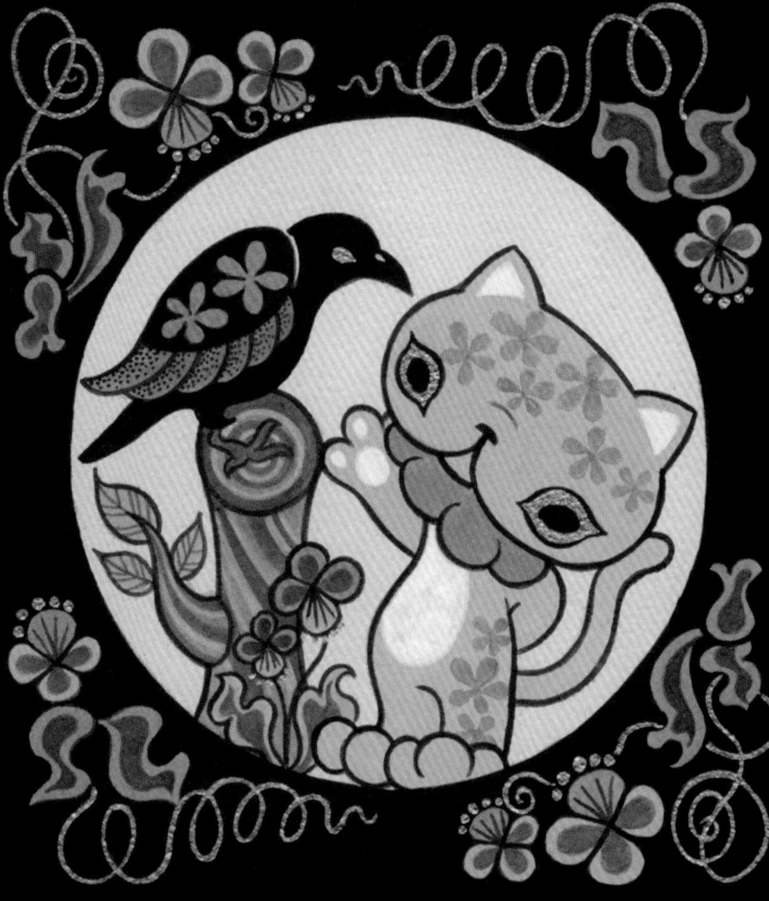

Stumbling around with hunger, Ravina came upon a cat that was chatting with a crow in the street. "Wow you are so good at speaking crow!" Ravina told him. "I also speak a bit of dog and squirrel," the cat replied, proudly.

Ravina told them that she was extremely hungry. She also asked why no one had any food and why there were no women in the town. The cat said that he could answer her questions and told her to follow him.

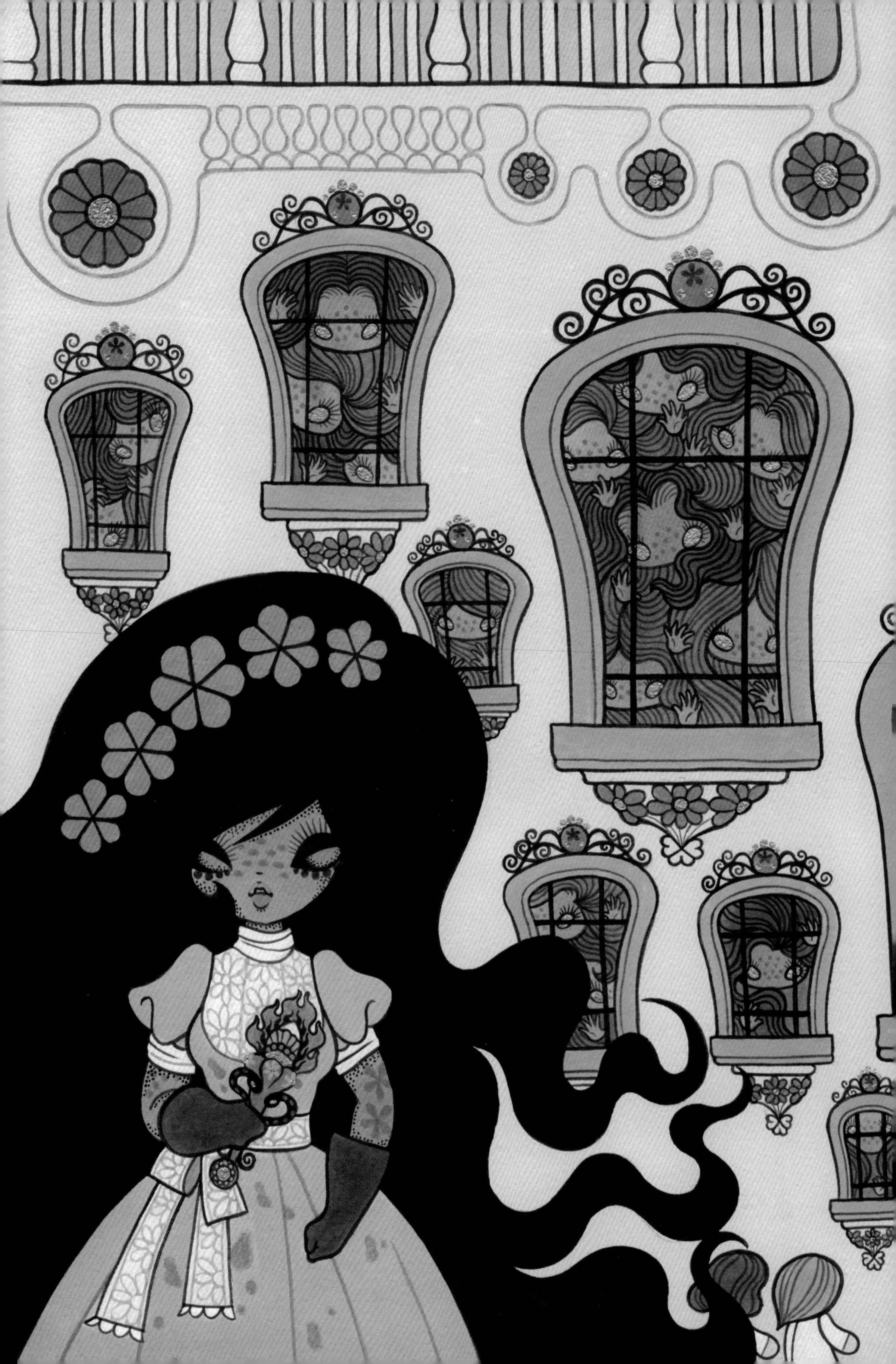

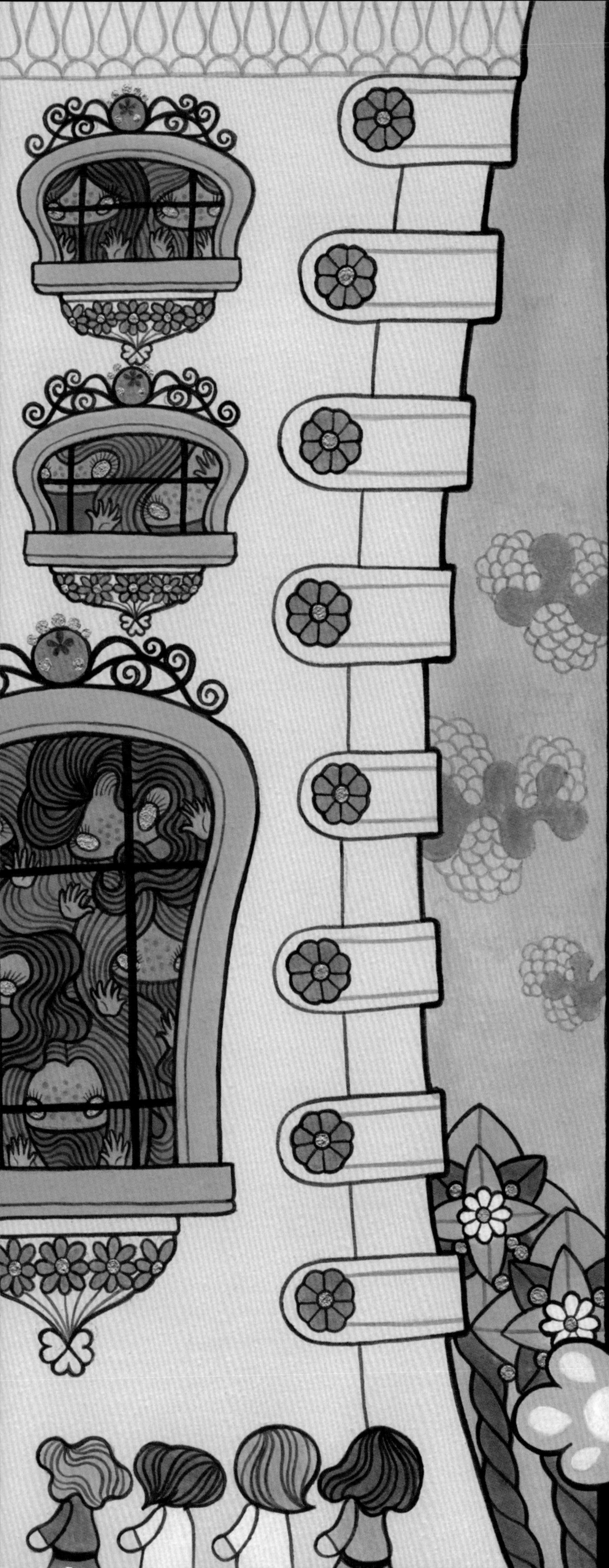

The cat brought Ravina to a large, old building where she saw many women cramped and suffering in the windows. Around the building, many men were looking up at the windows and crying. The cat explained...

"The king recently held a drinking contest. Any man who drank more than the king would win riches greater than they could possibly imagine. But if they lost, they would have to hand their wives over to the king. Because the prize was so great, every man in town entered the contest believing that they could win. But they underestimated how much the king could drink, and he bested them all. He took every one of their wives and put them here."

The cat went on to tell Ravina that the women held the keys to the town's food storage. None of the men knew how to cook anyway, which was why everyone was both sad and hungry!

Ravina visited each of the men to tell them that she could help free their wives if only they could spare her some alcohol.

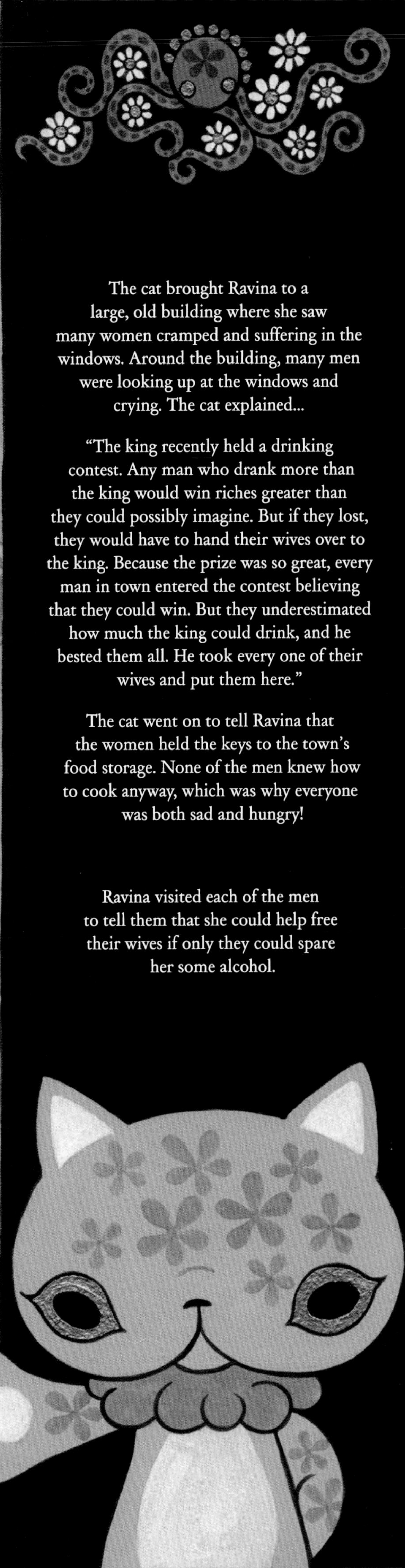

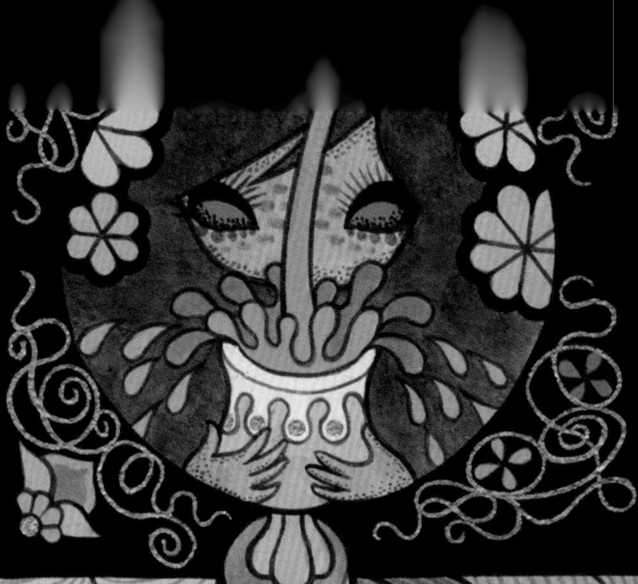

The owner of the spirits store gave her a big bottle of his wine. Ravina finished it at once.

She took out her wand and recited the magic words. The walls of the building disappeared and the wives escaped!

The guards of the building were so stunned to see it disappear that they could only stand and watch. The wives were very happy to be freed and they cooked large meals for Ravina.

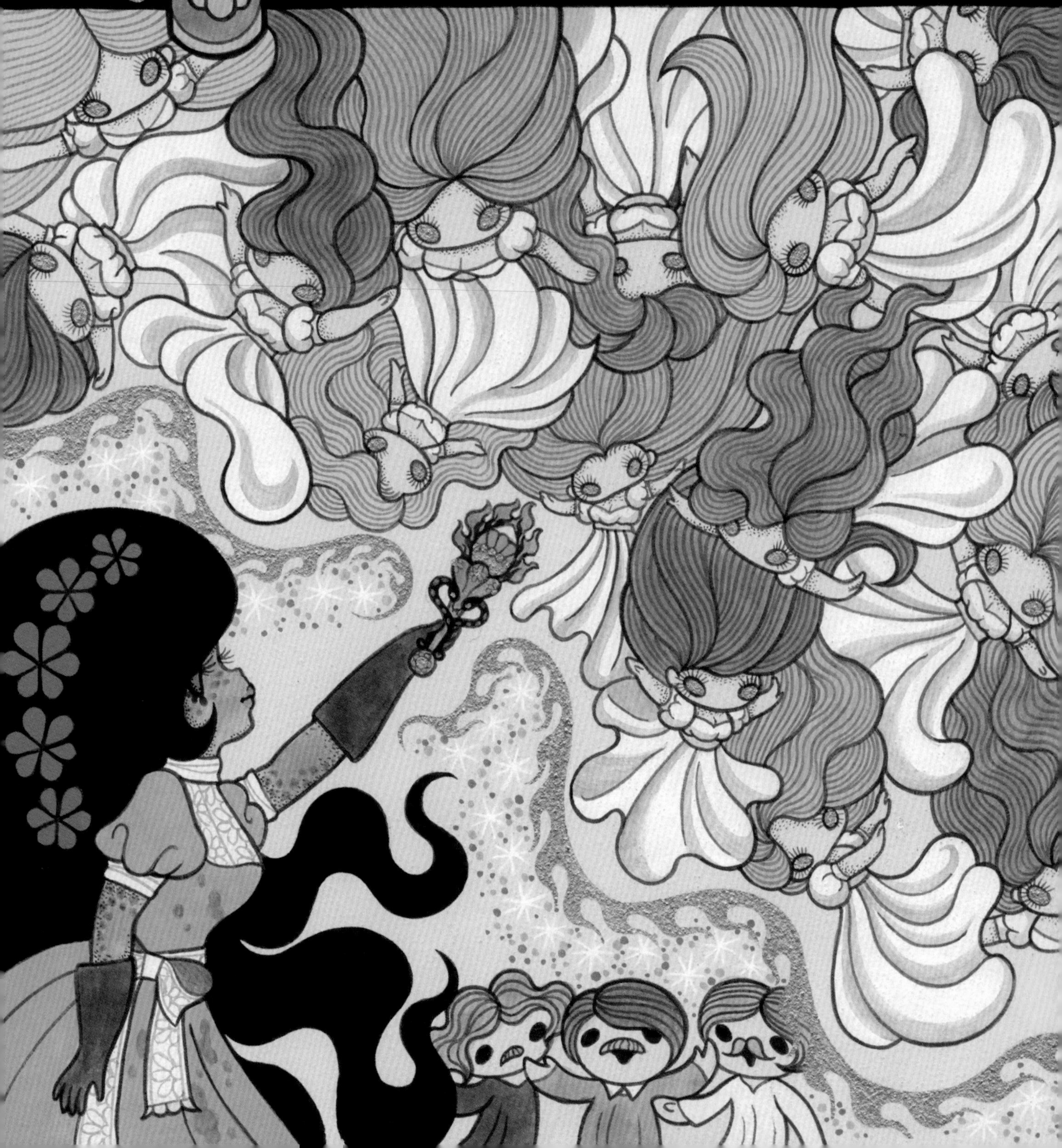

The king, hearing of
this drunk girl who caused
the building to vanish, was
so shocked that he forgot
all about being angry.
He demanded that this
curious woman be
brought before him.

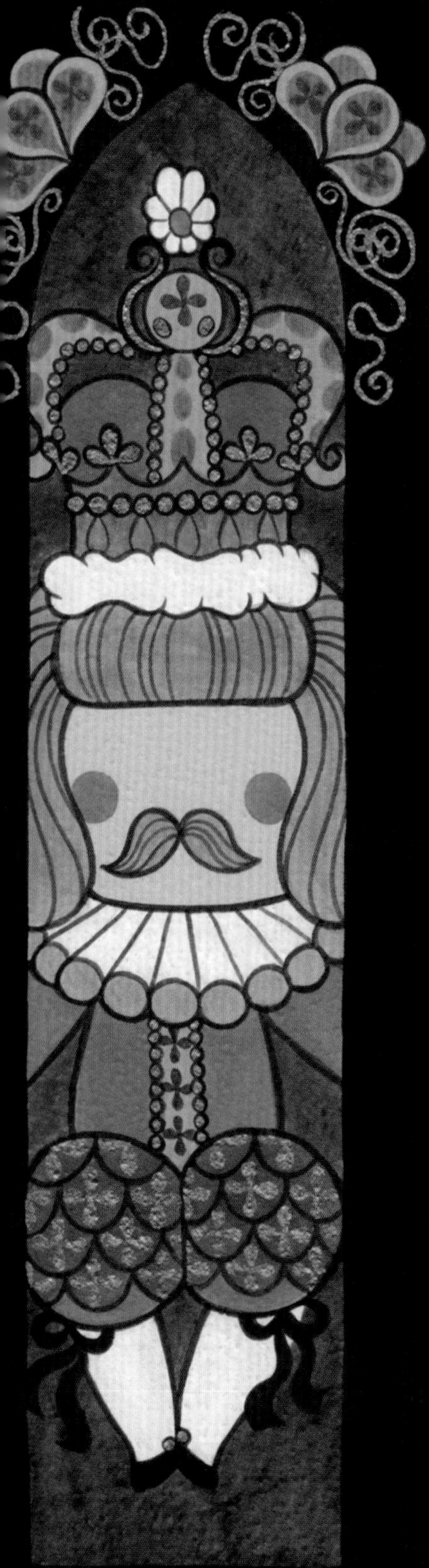

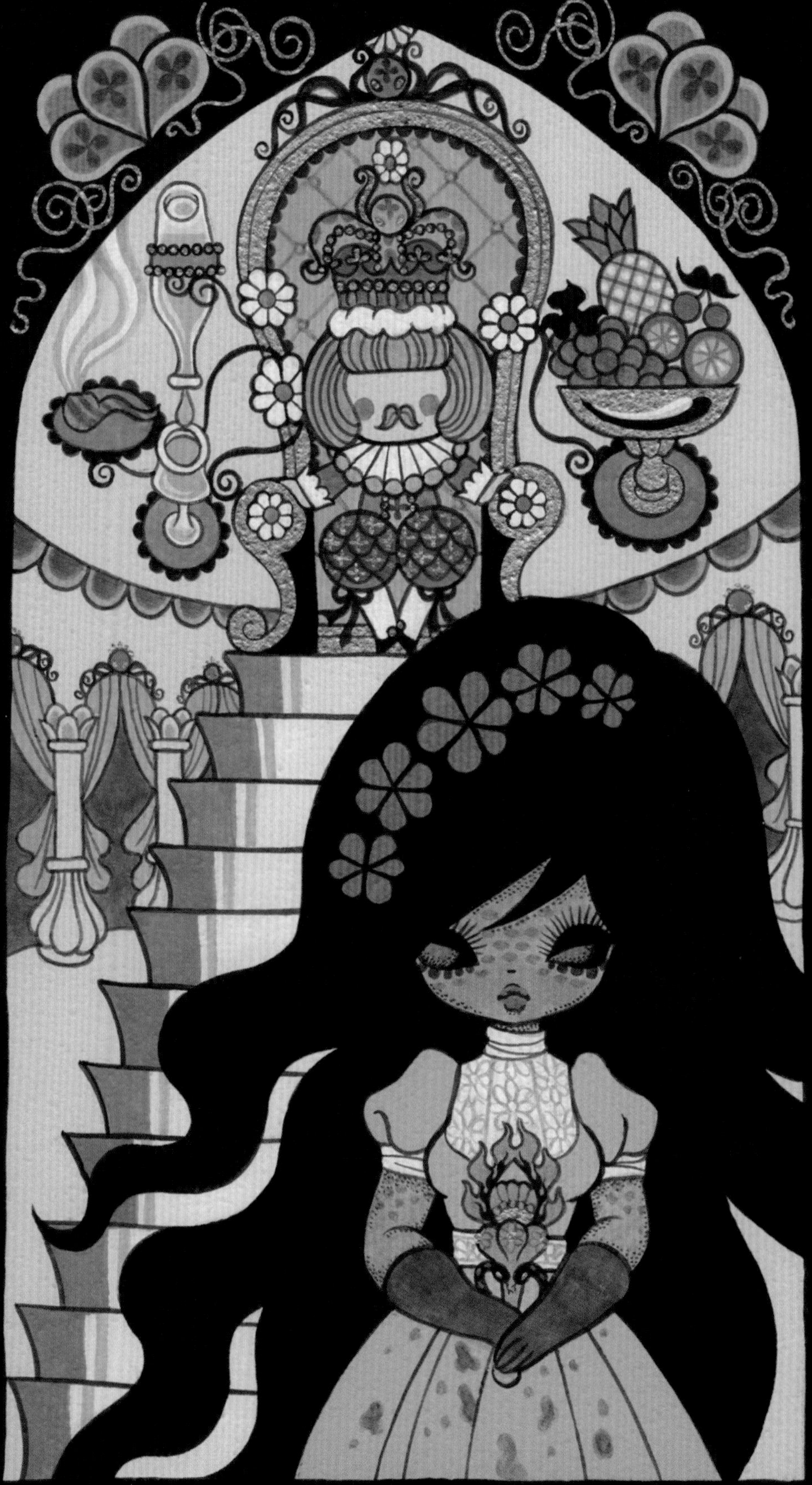

The guards found Ravina. They arrested her and brought her before the king.
The pompous king challenged Ravina to try and drink more than he could.

"If you don't take this challenge, you will merely go to jail.
If you win, all will be forgiven and you will be free to go and you will
also win the prize money I offered the men. But if you lose, you must
return to my building where you and all the women of my
kingdom will be trapped once more."

Realizing she had only one choice, Ravina agreed to the contest.

That night, in the castle's great hall, the competition began. Everyone in the town showed up to see if this girl could actually drink more than the king. Ravina took a sip of the liquor the king had chosen and exclaimed, "This is so good! I could keep drinking it forever!" The king and Ravina began to drink in earnest. As bottle after bottle fell empty to the floor, the crowd cheered and remarked:

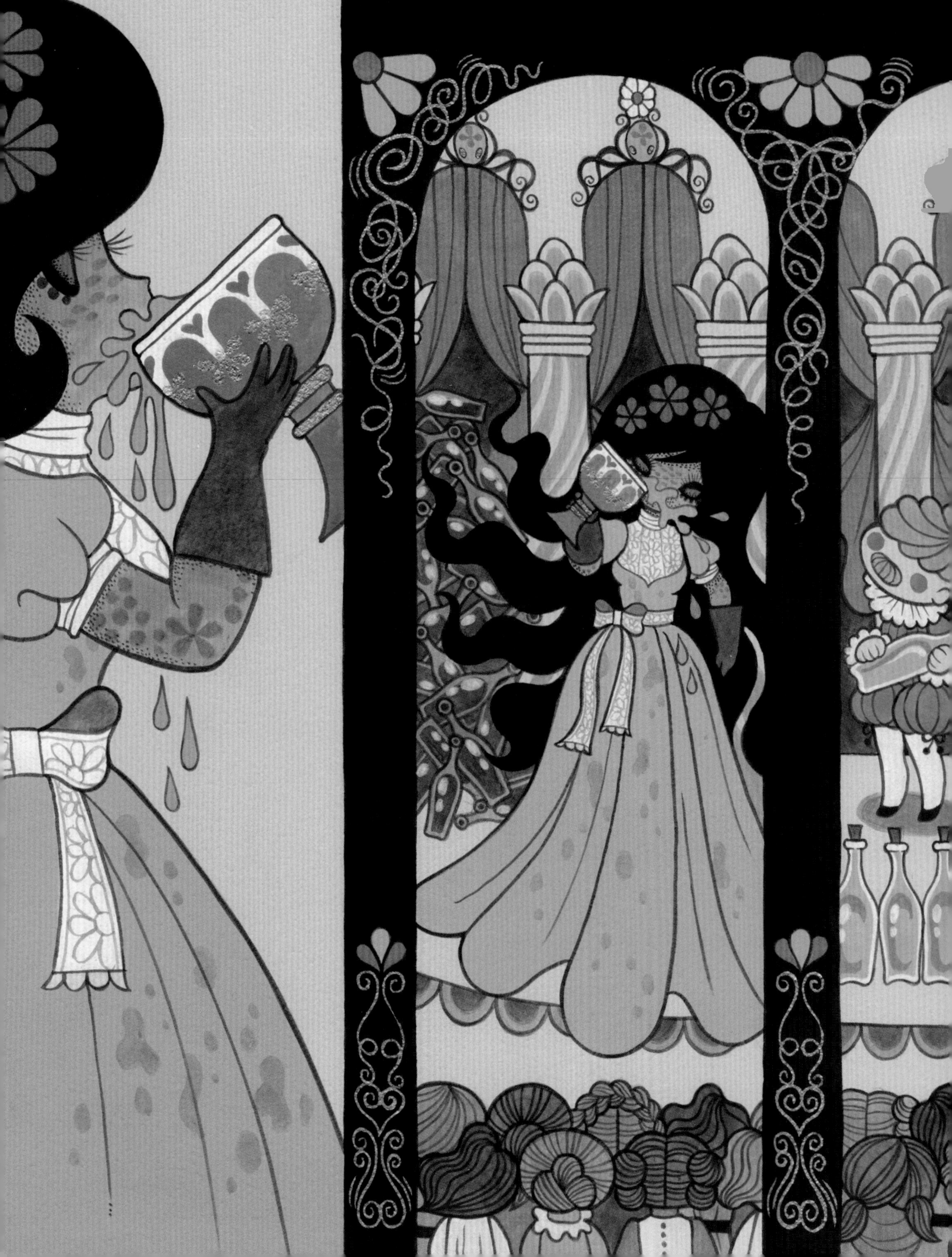

"The girl is actually keeping up with the king!"

However, watching among the excited villagers was the cat. He noticed something. The king was cheating! He was letting the liquor spill down into his big, frilly sleeve!

The cat came to Ravina and whispered to her of the king's deceit. Furious that he would cheat, Ravina took out the wand and waved it.

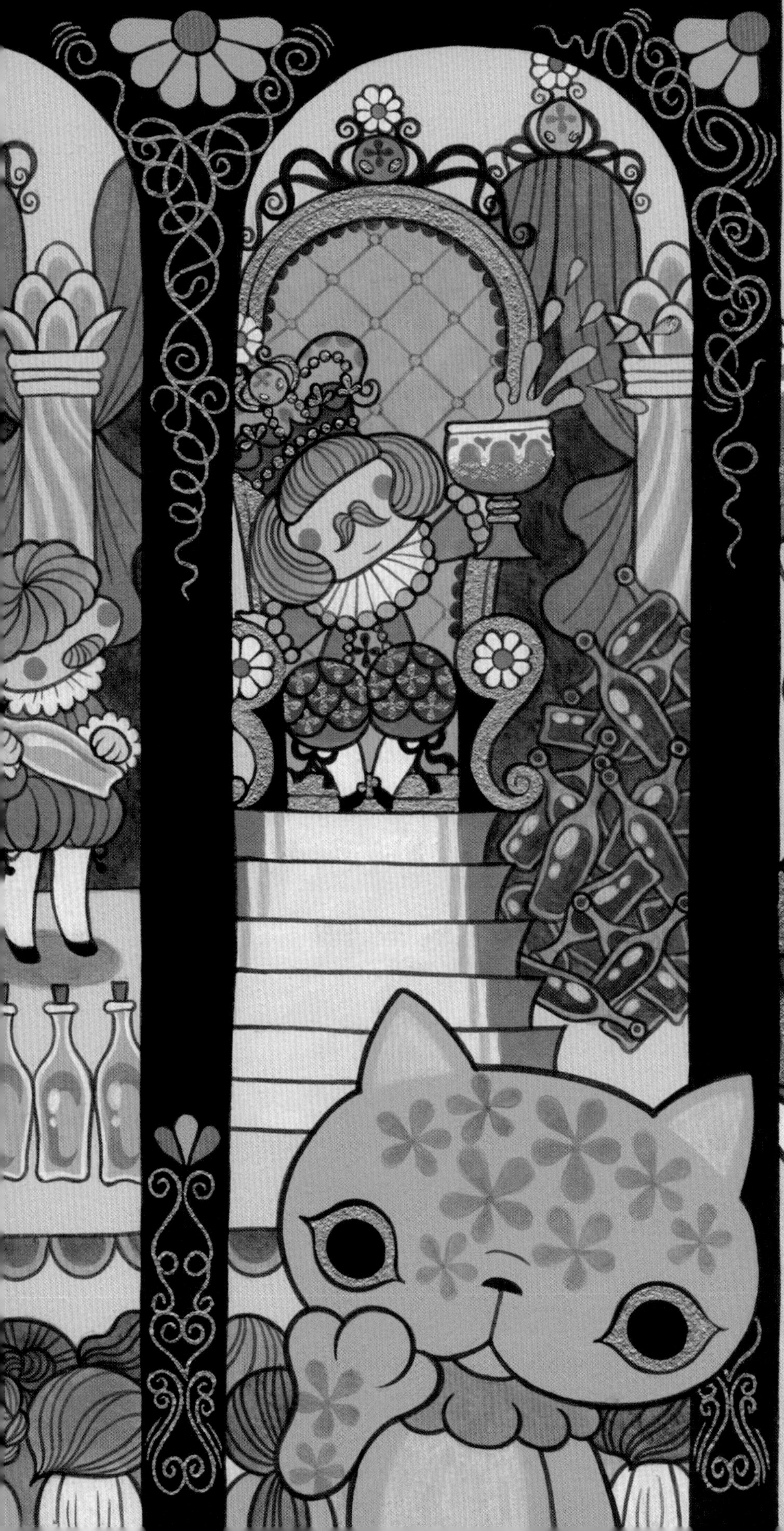

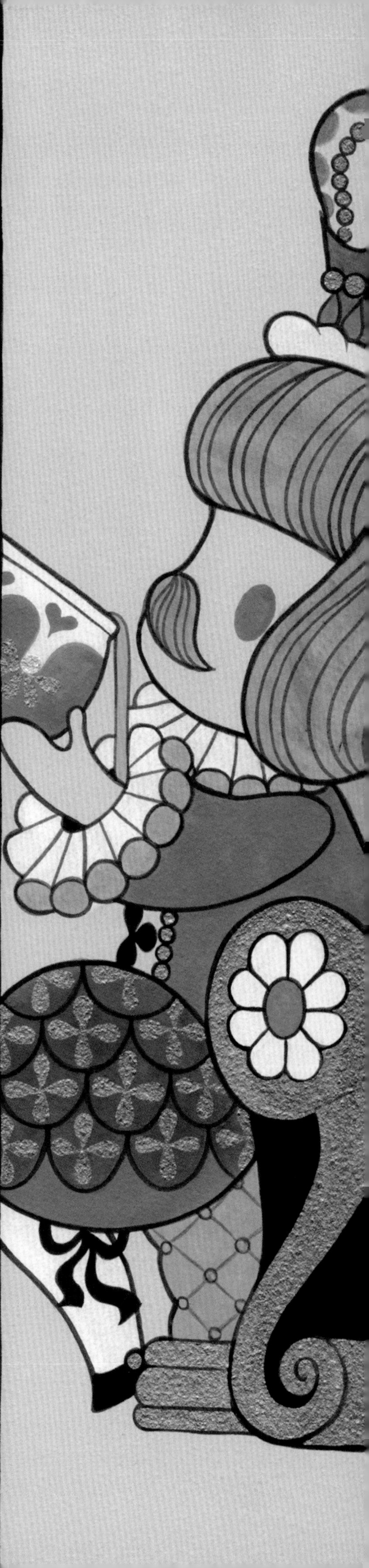

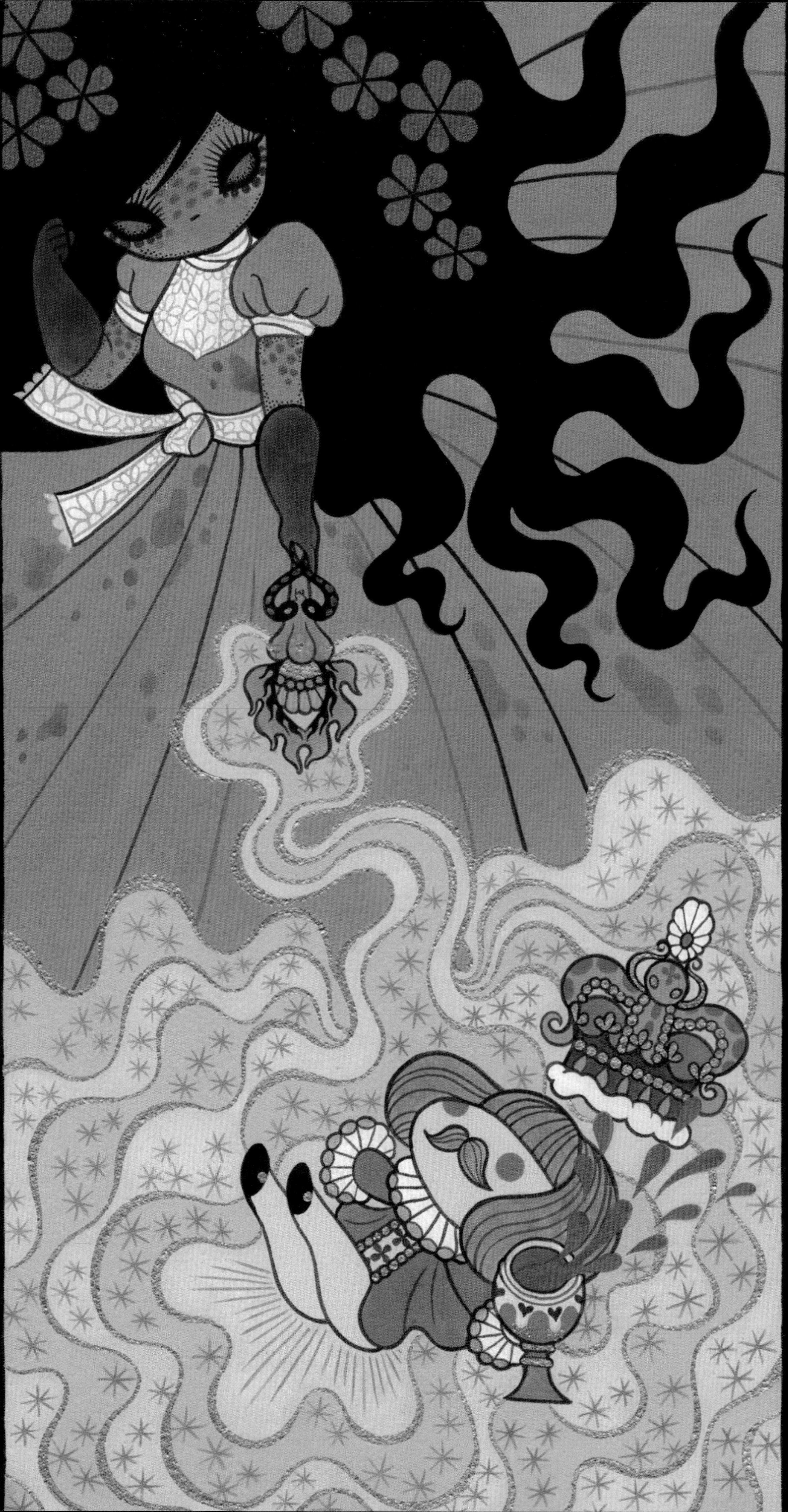

As she spoke the magic words, she made
the king's trousers disappear!

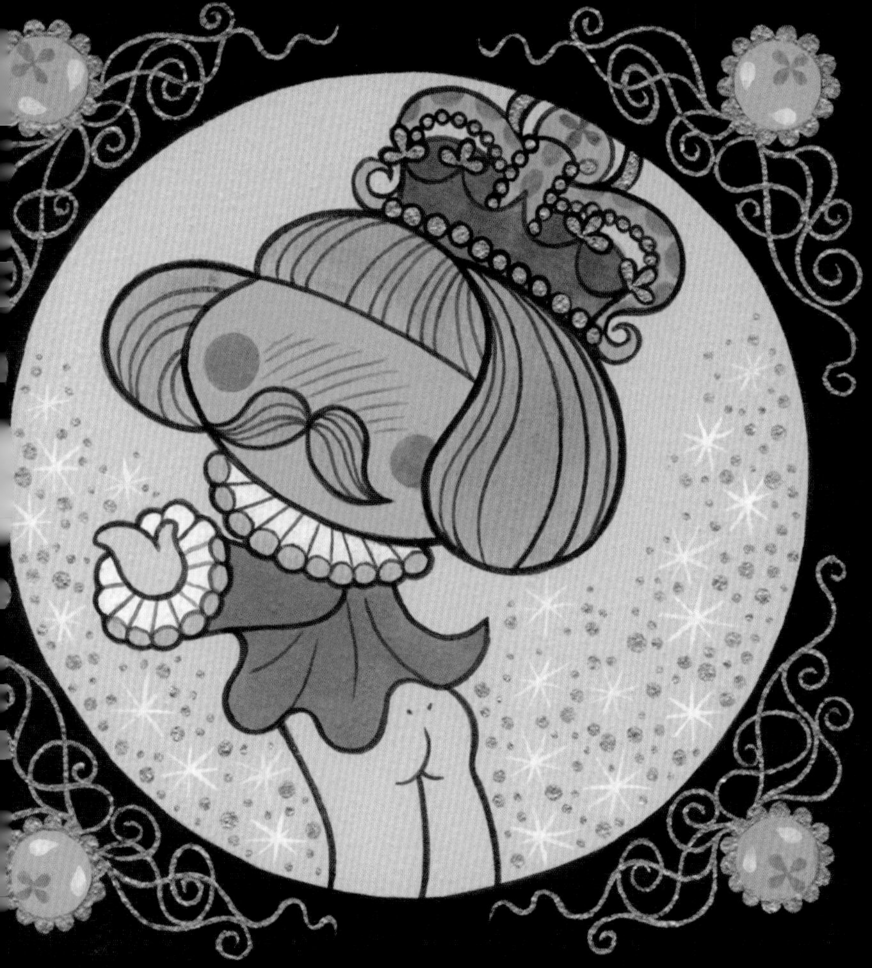

Upon seeing the king naked below the waist,
the townspeople all roared with laughter. Even the
guards were stifling their laughter until they heard the
king's orders. They grabbed Ravina, took away her
wand, and threw her into the castle's prison.

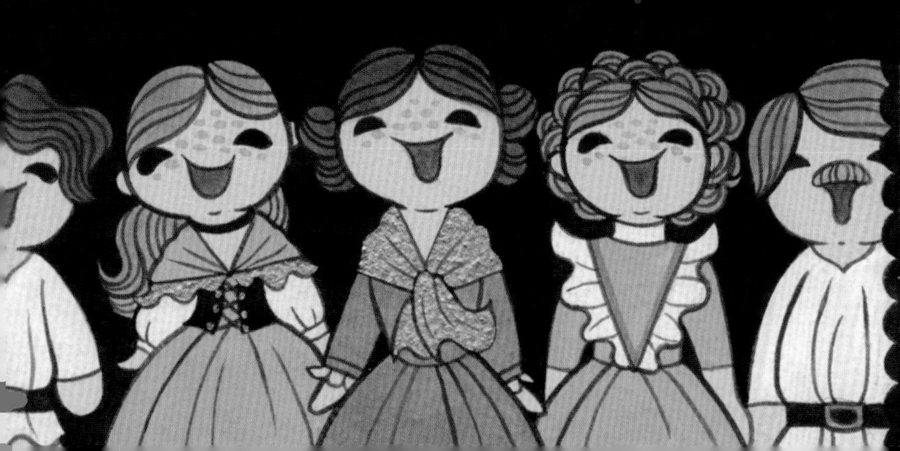

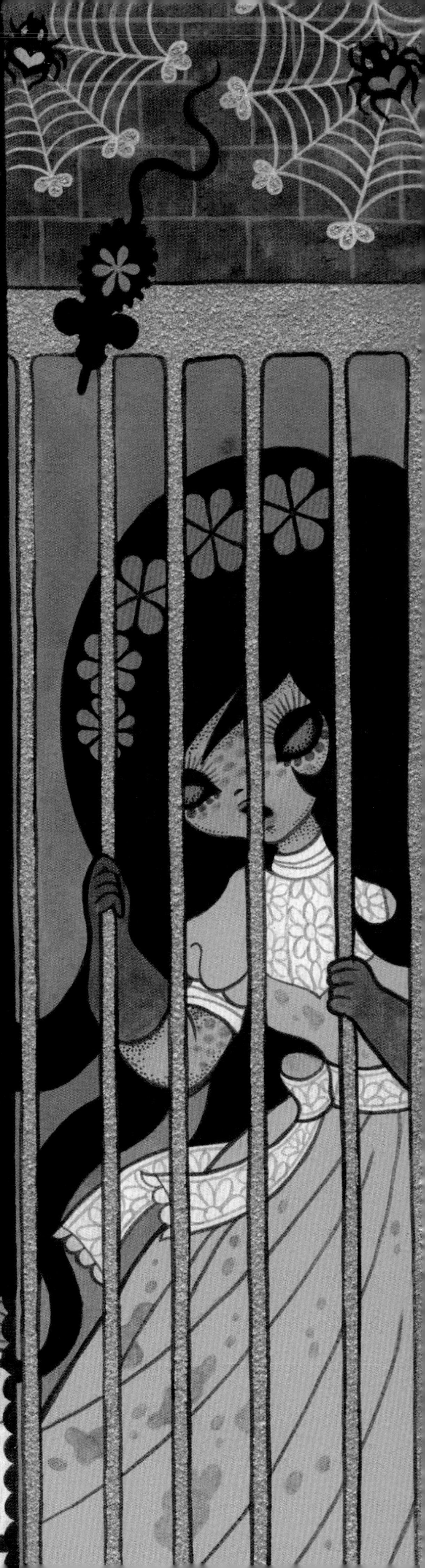

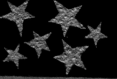

After the townspeople had left his castle, the king began to feel very angry and embarrassed. He was now desperate to recover his dignity. Soon, the word "witch" came across his mind. He had recently heard of "witch hunting" spreading through Europe.

"Maybe... that girl is... a witch?" The King said to his guards, "That explains how she could drink so much liquor and why my trousers suddenly vanished. And I heard that she came to the town using the power of flight. So..."

The guards were thrilled by the king's idea. They decided to interrogate Ravina to find out if she was indeed a witch.

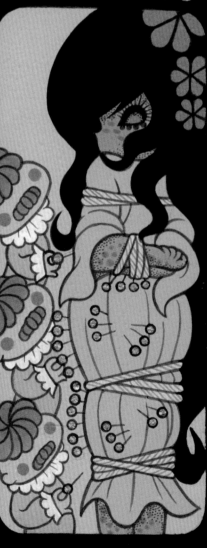

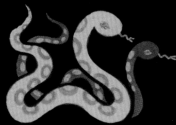

The guards took Ravina outside and tortured her in every manner. They bound her, soaked her in water, and put needles all over her body. As the guards stuck Ravina, she thought of the old woman who gave her the wand. Ravina feared that she might die just as she had. But despite the long hours of torture, the guards could not come to a conclusion. None of them really knew how to tell if someone was a witch or not. Eventually, the guards all became tired and sleepy. They decided to postpone the interrogation and throw Ravina back in jail for the night.

Even though she was exhausted and imprisoned,
Ravina was still happy to be alive. Her fate was unknown.
As she wondered what more could be done to her,
she heard a noise at the window. It was the cat.
"Are you alright?" he asked.

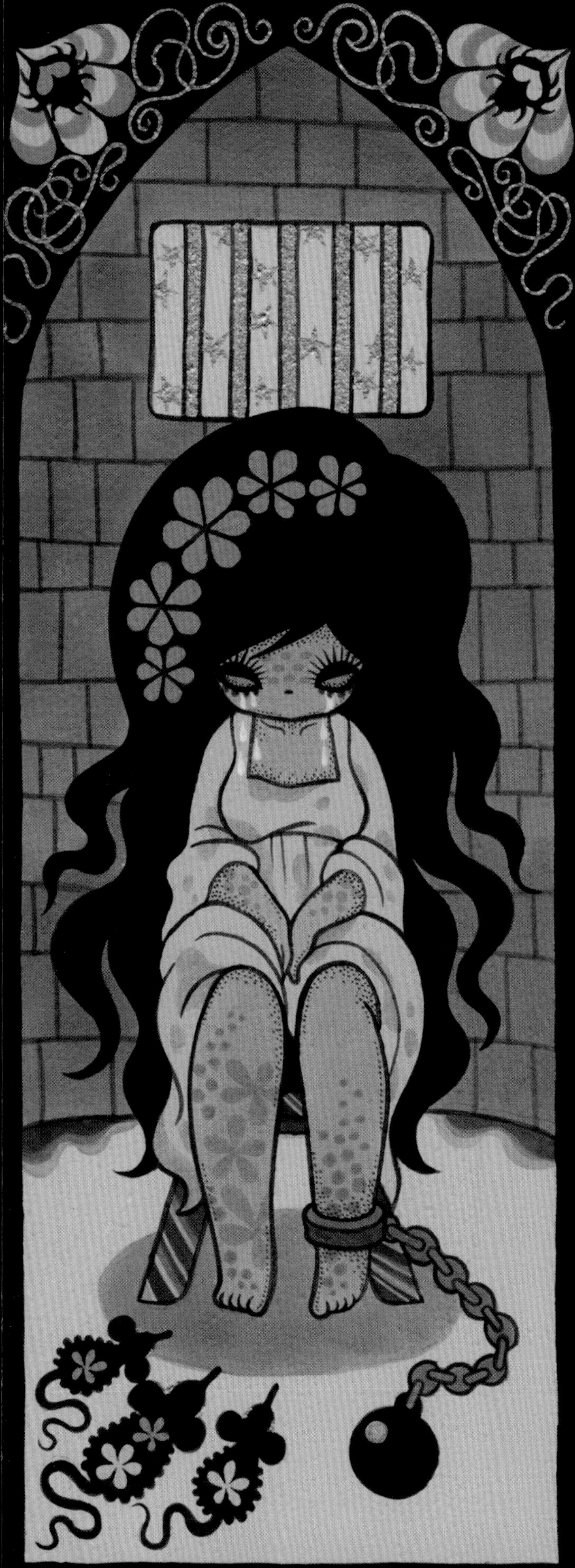

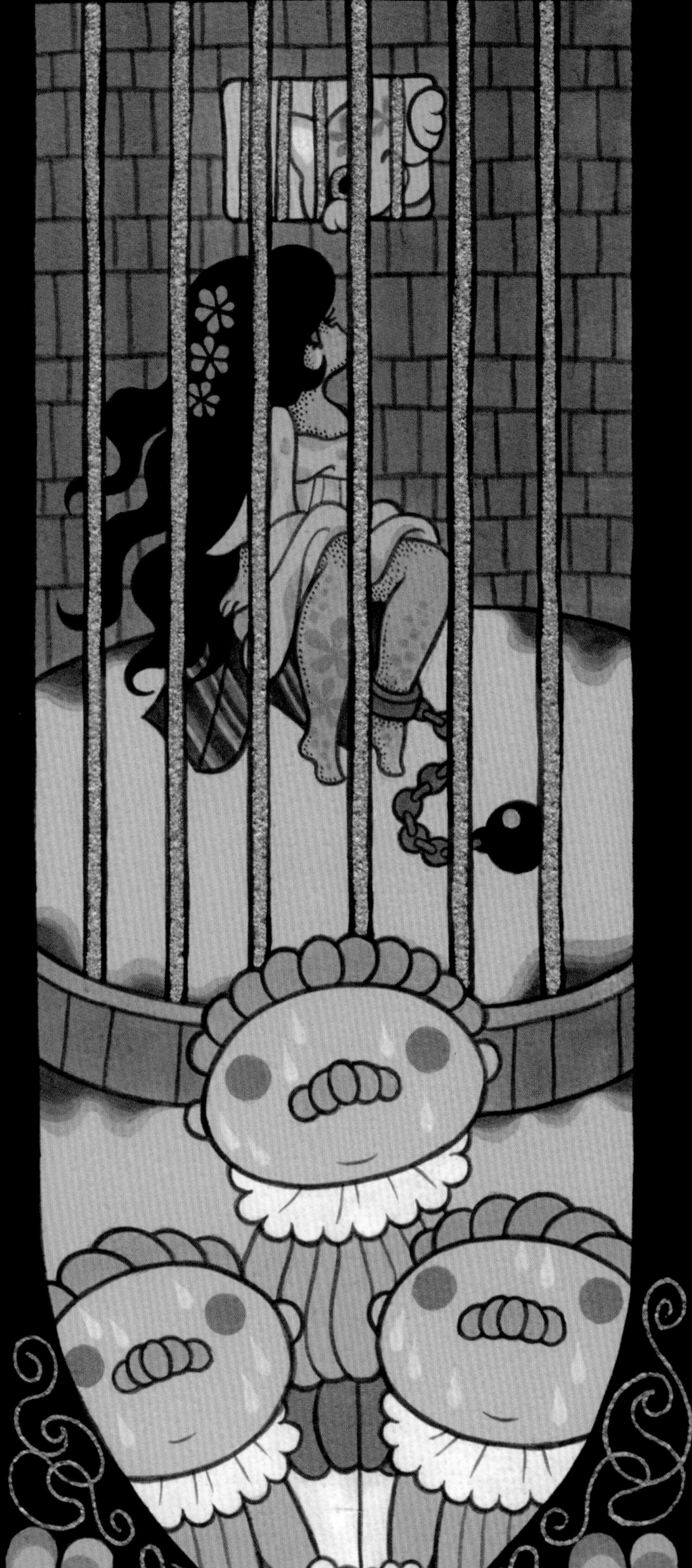

Ravina began to answer, and one of the guards came to investigate the sounds coming from her cell. Upon seeing Ravina and the cat talking to each other in a strange language, he was frightened.

He ran immediately to the king and exclaimed, "She IS a witch!" Satisfied at once with this proof, the king declared that Ravina was to be burned to death at once.

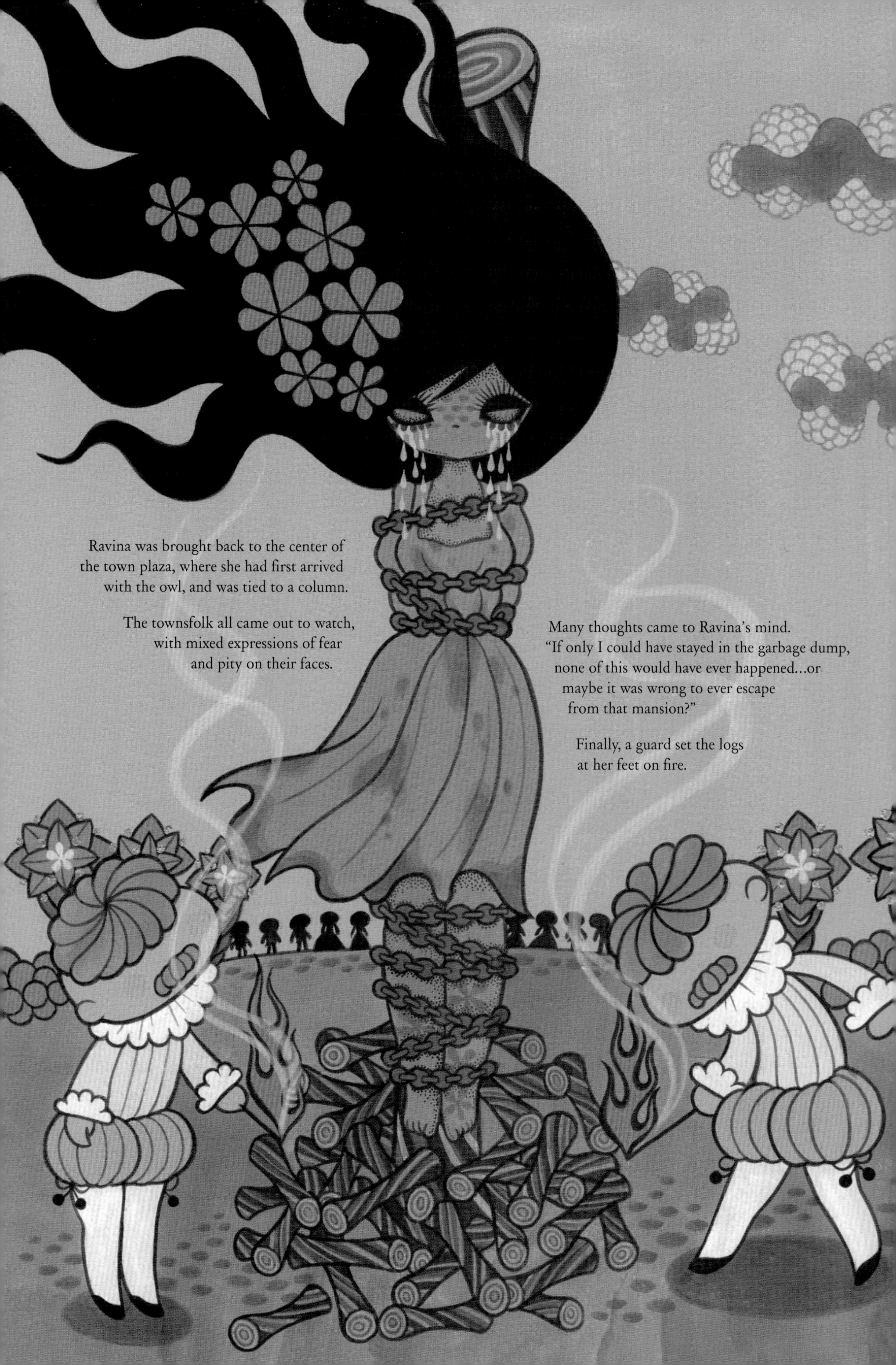

Ravina was brought back to the center of the town plaza, where she had first arrived with the owl, and was tied to a column.

The townsfolk all came out to watch, with mixed expressions of fear and pity on their faces.

Many thoughts came to Ravina's mind. "If only I could have stayed in the garbage dump, none of this would have ever happened…or maybe it was wrong to ever escape from that mansion?"

Finally, a guard set the logs at her feet on fire.

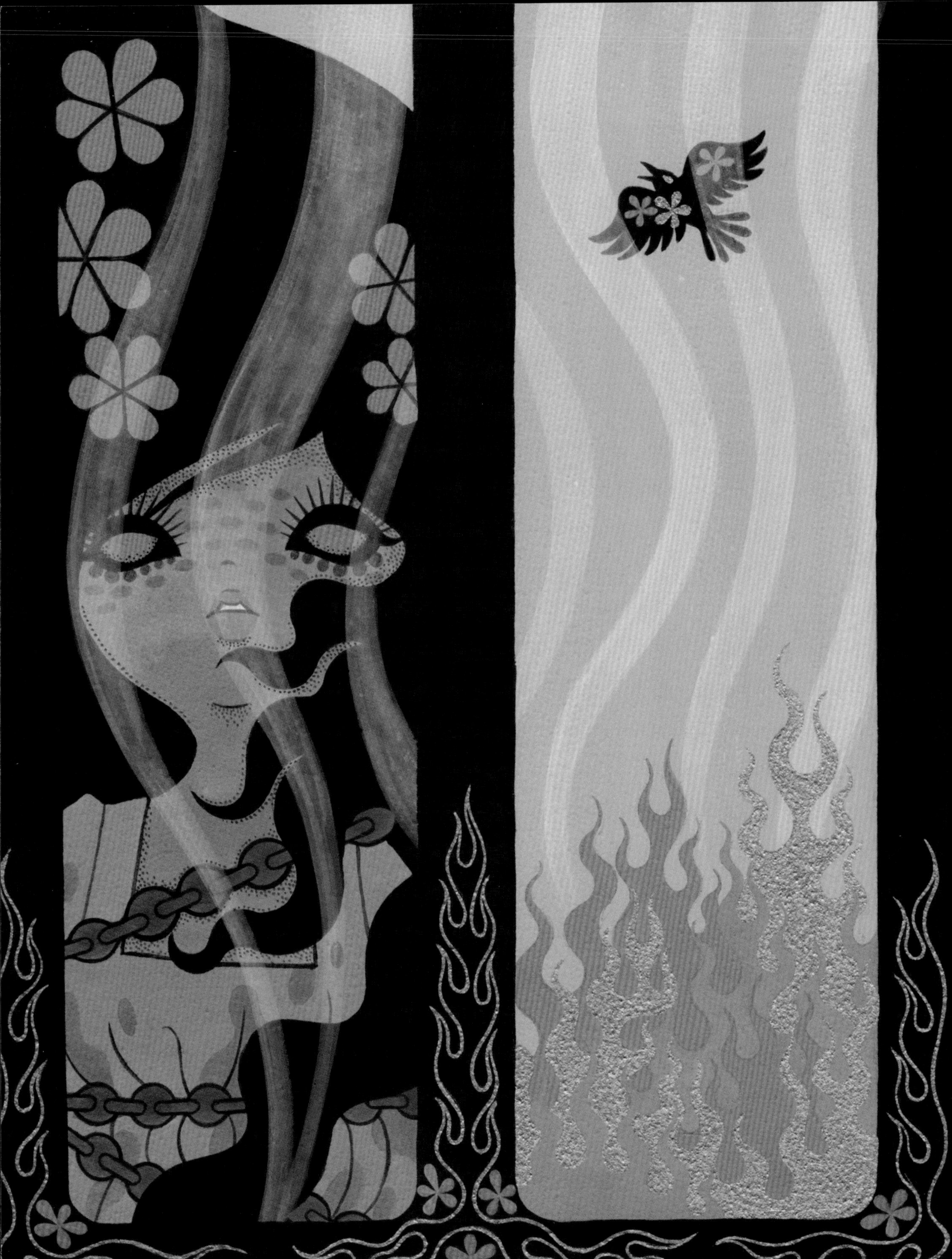

As her feet began to feel the scorching heat, Ravina looked up helplessly.
Through the smoke rising up around her, she saw a crow flying in the sky.

And then, the people in the plaza heard Ravina cry out something
in a language they could not understand.

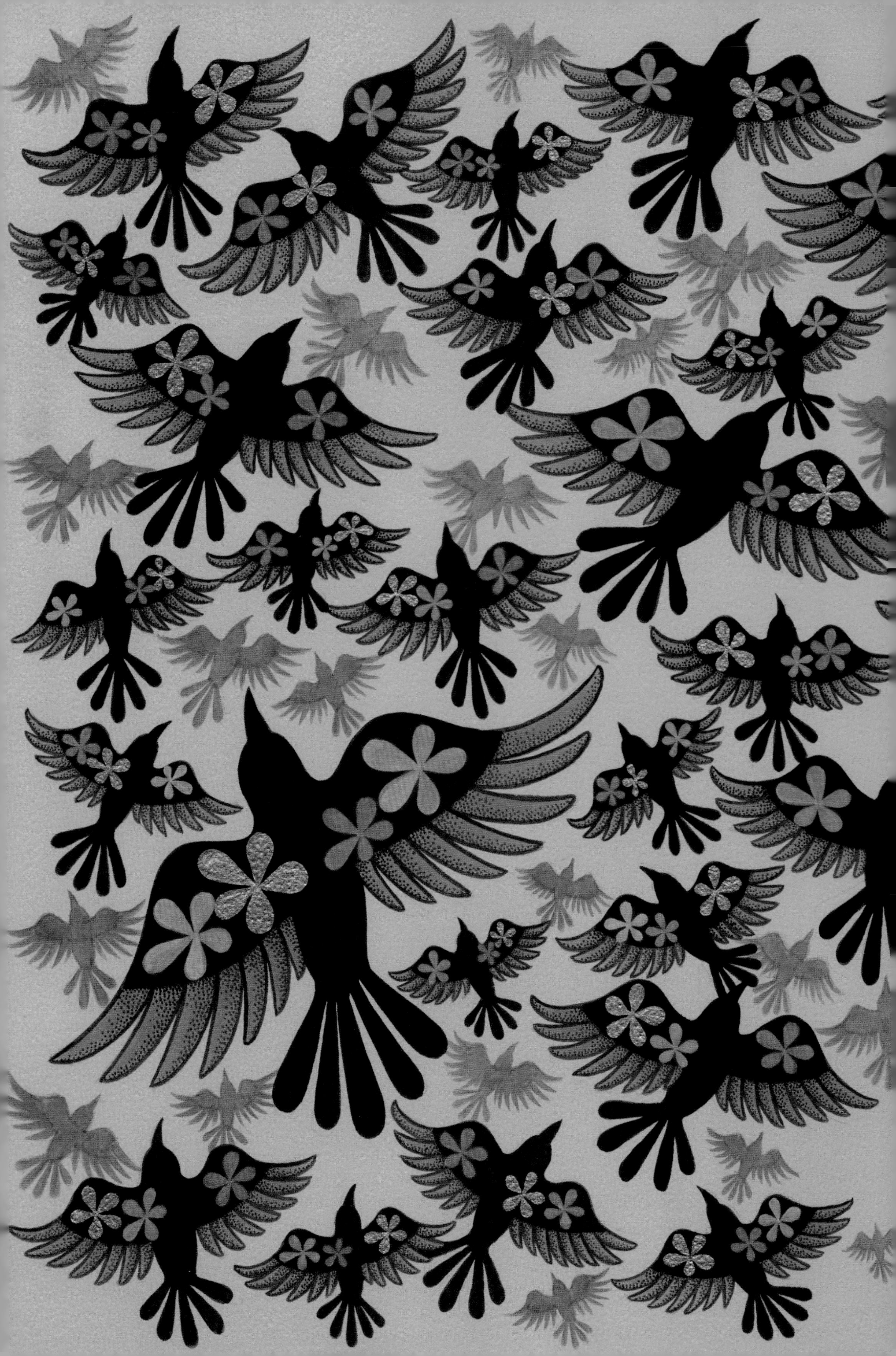

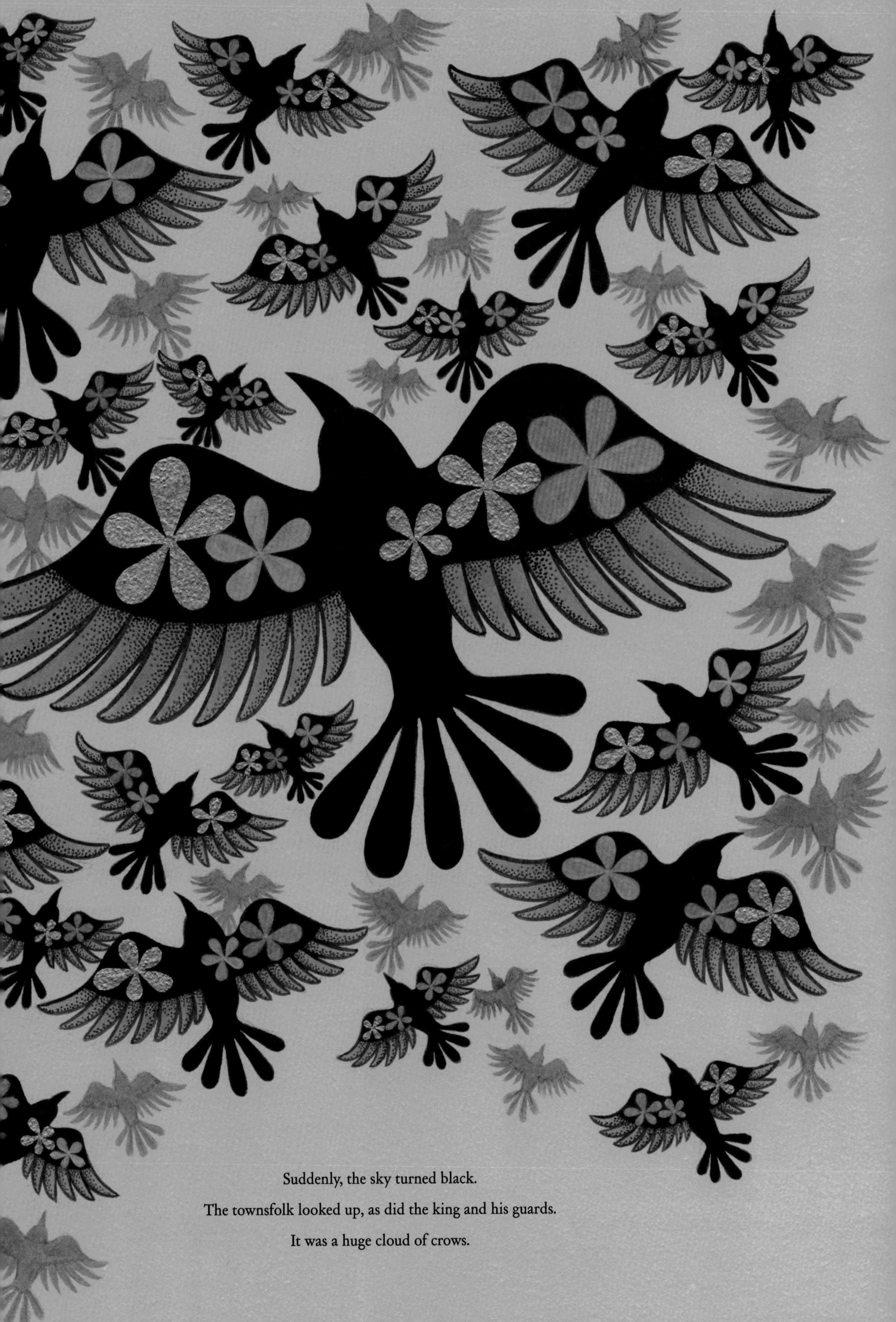

Suddenly, the sky turned black.

The townsfolk looked up, as did the king and his guards.

It was a huge cloud of crows.

They had heard Ravina's cries for help. As the king and his subjects ran around in fright, the crows swooped down and bit at the chains binding Ravina to the column. Freeing her, they lifted Ravina from the fire and took to the sky.

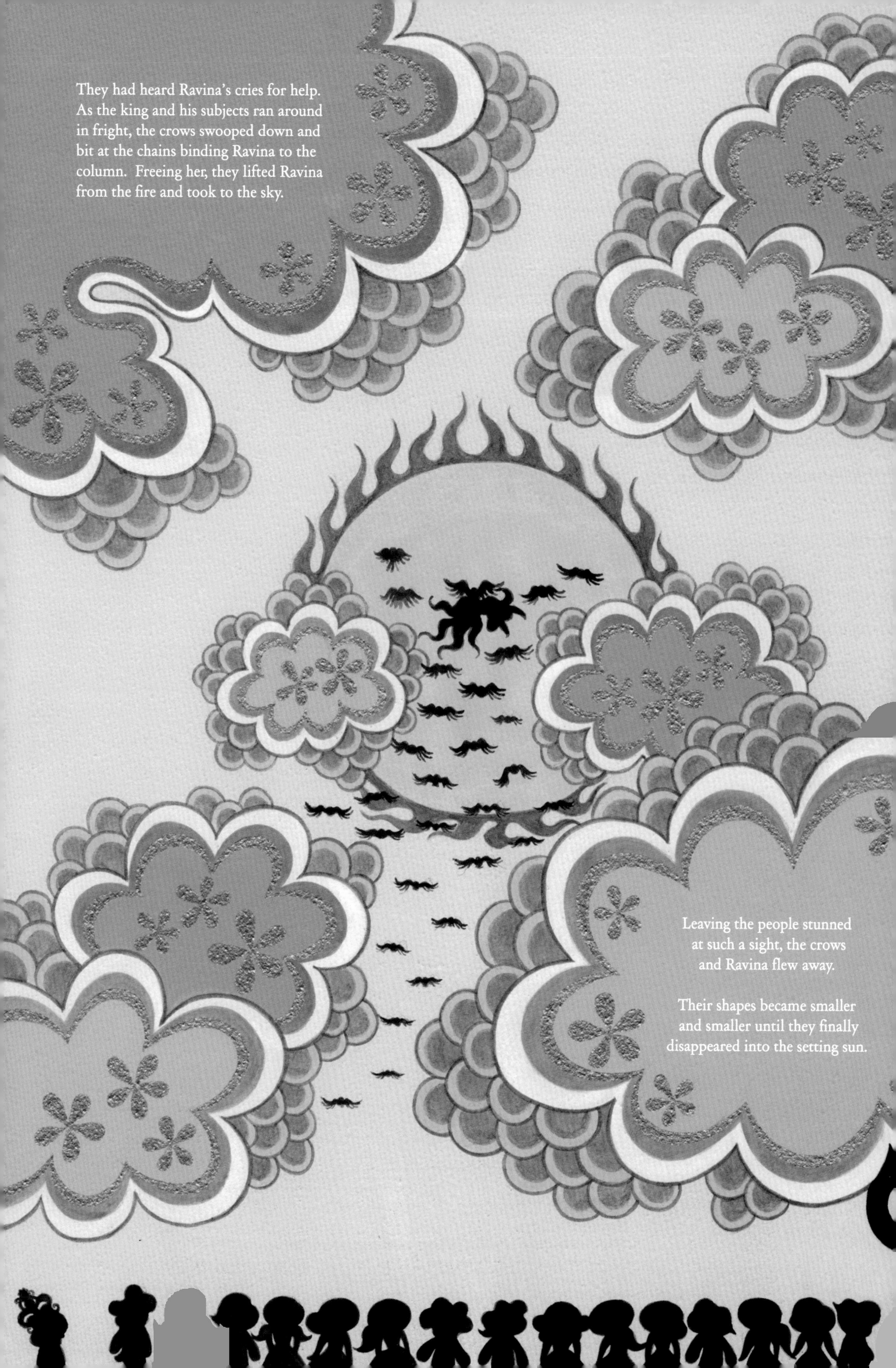

Leaving the people stunned at such a sight, the crows and Ravina flew away.

Their shapes became smaller and smaller until they finally disappeared into the setting sun.

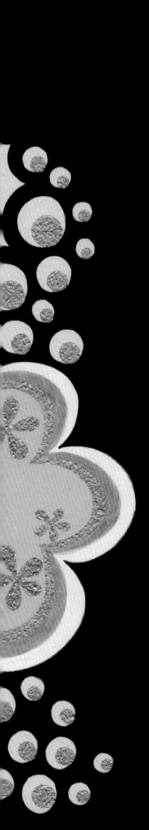

*And that was the last anyone ever saw
or heard of the girl named Ravina...*

The End

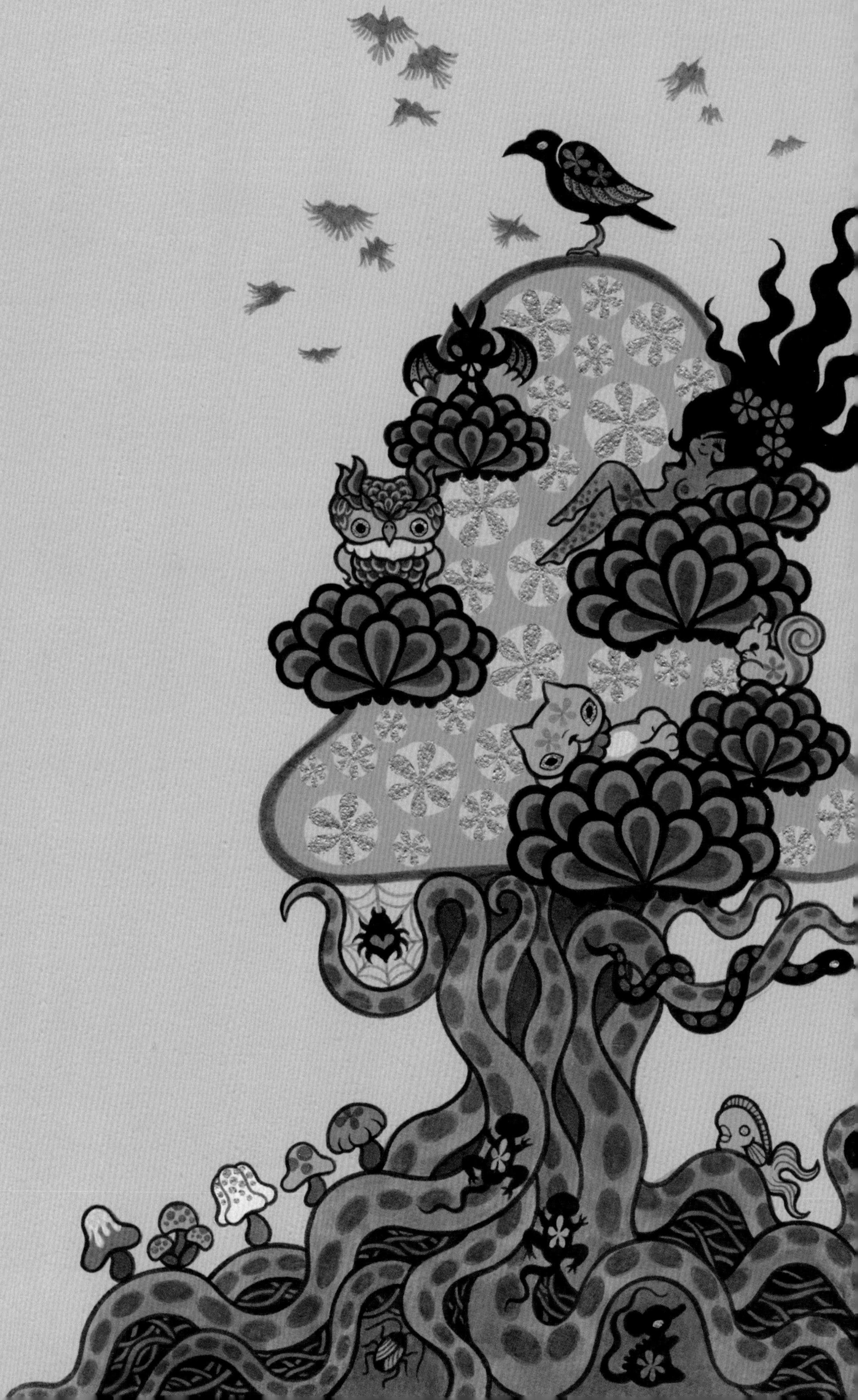

Junko Mizuno...

...was born in Tokyo, on the 27th of May, 1973.

In 1996, Junko self-published a book called *MINA animal DX*, which was critically acclaimed in the Japanese publishing world.

Shortly after, she made her debut as an author, illustrator, and graphic designer of comics.

Entirely self-taught, she became a recognised master in the field, whose unique style blends femininity, eroticism, and fantasy.

www.MIZUNO-JUNKO.com.

Books in French

2010 *Pilou, l'Apprenti Gigolo, vol. 1* * Éditions IMHO - France

2006 *Hell Babies Upgraded* * Éditions Treville - Japan
Pure Trance * Éditions IMHO - France

2005 *La Petite Sirène* * Éditions IMHO - France

2004 *Cinderella* * Éditions IMHO - France

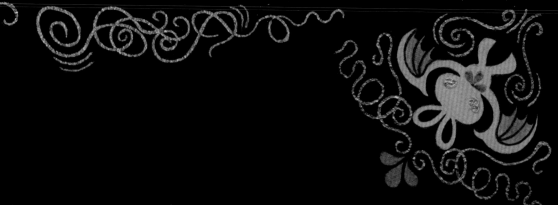

Gallery Exhibitions (selected list)

2013   *Rising* * Nucleus Gallery - Alhambra - USA

2012   *Euphoria* * La Luz De Jesus Gallery - Los Angeles - USA
        Venus Cake   Magic Pony | Narwhal Art Projects - Toronto
        Ontario - Canada

2010   *Fujiyama Girls* * Mondo Bizzarro Gallery - Rome - Italy

2009   *Desert Women* * Roq La Rue Gallery - Seattle - USA

2007   *Heart Throb* * Merry Karnowsky Gallery - Los Angeles - USA

2006   *The Juxtapoz Annual Group Show '06* * OX-OP Gallery
        Minneapolis - USA

2005   *The Pony Project* * Milk Gallery - New York - USA

1998   *Hell Babies* * Art Wads Gallery - Tokyo - Japan

Other Exhibitions (selected list)

2011   *Live painting | Artist-in-residence* * Kidrobot shop
        in Cosmopolitan Hotel - Las Vegas - USA

        Pinatarama * Museum of Modern Art - Mexico

2010   *Small Gift - Sanrio's 50th Anniversary Art Show* * Barker Hangar
        Santa Monica - USA

        *SugiPOP : The Influence of Anime and Manga on Contemporary
        Art* * Portsmouth Museum Of Art - USA

2008   *Krazy! The Delirious World of Anime, Comics, Video Games, Art*
        Vancouver Art Gallery - Vancouver - Canada & Japan Society
         Gallery - New York - USA

2006   *Fumetto International* * Triennale di Milano - Italy

Collection Editor
Lizzie Kaye

Senior Comics Editor
Andrew James

Titan Comics Editorial
Tom Williams, Jessica Burton & Amoona Saohin

Production Manager
Obi Onuora

Production Supervisor
Jackie Flook

Production Assistant
Peter James

Senior Sales Manager
Steve Tothill

Direct Sales and Marketing Manager
Ricky Claydon

Brand Manager
Chris Thompson

Publishing Manager
Darryl Tothill

Publishing Director
Chris Teather

Operations Director
Leigh Baulch

Executive Director
Vivian Cheung

Publisher
Nick Landau

A collection directed by Barbara Canepa and Clotilde Vu

Created by : Junko Mizuno,
with help from Adeline Richet-Lartigue

Logotype 'Venusdea' : Matteo De Longis
Translation from Japanese to English : C.B. Cebulski,
Patrick Macias and Jason Thompson

ISBN: 9781785858536

Published by Titan Comics
A division of Titan Publishing Group Ltd.
144 Southwark St. London SE1 0UP

© ÉDITIONS SOLEIL – VENUSDEA / MIZUNO
http://www.mizuno-junko.com

A CIP catalogue record for this title is available from the British Library.

First edition: May 2017

Printed in China.